CROCHET
SOUTHWEST *Spirit*

OVER 20 BOHEMIAN
PATTERNS INSPIRED
BY THE AMERICAN
SOUTHWEST

SUSAN KENNEDY

DAVID & CHARLES
—PUBLISHING—

www.davidandcharles.com

CONTENTS

INTRODUCTION

Welcome to the wilderness and freedom of the American southwest! *Crochet Southwest Spirit* offers a laid-back bohemian style inspired by natural landscapes that will bring a breath of fresh air to your crochet repertoire. You'll feel the expansiveness of wide-open spaces and deep turquoise skies as you create stunning work from this unique collection of crochet patterns. *Crochet Southwest Spirit* celebrates the character and spirit of this area, drawing inspiration from its ancient sacred places and vivid spring blooms in the meadows. Peaceful color palettes drawn from the mountains, mesas, deserts, valleys, forests, rivers, and rock formations of the southwest bring a relaxed vibe to these beginner and intermediate patterns.

The Four Corners

I am blessed to be surrounded by beautiful geography, living in the gorgeous San Juan mountains near Durango, Colorado. The area where Colorado, Utah, New Mexico, and Arizona meet is called the Four Corners. My home is in the southwest corner of Colorado where the San Juan National Forest meets the Pine River valley. You won't find any big cities, traffic, yarn stores, or fast-food restaurants here. Just tranquil mountains covered in pine, blue spruce, and aspen trees and plenty of room to breathe. The landscapes of the Four Corners have inspired artists for millennia, from its lush forests and rushing rivers to dry, cactus-filled mesas and dusty trails. Like generations of crafters before me, my experiences in the natural world around me find their way into my creative work. The ideas for many of the projects in this book, such as the Sedona Knot Cushion, the Bears Ears Fringed Pillow, and the Valley of Dreams Blanket, were born after visiting unique places in the Four Corners. Gratitude and respect for the land, environment, and historical crafting traditions of the area led me to choose natural fiber yarn over synthetics for this collection.

The Joy of Crochet

I learned to crochet as an adult after earning degrees in math and neuroscience and becoming a mother. My love of math and geometry inspire me to make interesting patterns that are as effortless as possible to stitch. Patterns don't have to be complicated to be beautiful. The projects in this book make the most of the meditative repetition and soothing rhythm of crocheting for maximum enjoyment and satisfaction. Many of them would be lovely to create while unwinding over a weekend. My passion is making modern boho home décor inspired by nature, that is as practical and durable as it is beautiful. You'll find blankets, pillows, rugs, baskets, towels, wall hangings, wraps, and tote bags in this collection. Here, simple serape-style stripes are right at home next to more intricate southwestern tapestry crochet patterns.

My favorite way to celebrate the completion of a crochet project is to take it outside for a quick photo. I love to twirl around with a newly finished blanket and watch the tassels and fringe come alive while one of my sons snaps a photo. I invite you to take your finished projects out for a twirl to celebrate your creativity!

Happy crocheting,

Susan

SOUTHWEST TEXTILE TRADITIONS

As an artist in the San Juan mountains of southwest Colorado, I honor the Ute, Pueblo, and Diné Navajo people as the traditional custodians of the land I live on. I hold the fiber arts traditions carried on by generations of Southern Ute, Ute Mountain, Diné Navajo, and Hopi families in great respect, and share what I know about the history of the artists who came before me as a way to pay my respects, spread southwestern culture, and serve my community.

"When you learn something from people, or from a culture, you accept it as a gift, and it is your lifelong commitment to preserve it and build on it."

Yo-Yo Ma

One thing I enjoy about living in the southwest is listening to stories and learning about traditions from my Southern Ute and Diné Navajo neighbors. The traditions in these cultures are rooted in the cycles of the seasons and the interconnectedness of all living things. These stories have changed the way I see our area, its history, and its seasonal changes, giving me a new view that inspires new ideas. Several of the projects in this book have connections to local lore and to families that have been raising sheep and making yarn in the southwest for generations.

Navajo Weaving

The Navajo Nation or *Diné Bikéyah* covers over 27,000 square miles (69,930 km²) of the Four Corners area. Diné is the name Navajo people call themselves. The Four Corners area has been famous for the beautiful woven rugs and blankets created by Diné people for hundreds of years. Diné weaving uses an upright loom with no moving parts, creating flat-woven textiles often made with naturally dyed wool. Diné weaving is a sacred art, with the top beam of the loom representing the sky, the bottom bar representing Mother Earth, the warp representing rain, and the tension cord representing lightning.

A beautiful diversity of designs as unique as each weaver continue to be treasured today. Some traditional designs include Two Gray Hills, Teec Nos Pos, Ganado, Wide Ruins, Chinle, Klagetoh, Yei be Chei, Eye Dazzler, and Red Mesa. Diné textile culture is active and evolving, with weavers like Roy Kady teaching the next generation to carry traditions forward. My appreciation for the artistry of indigenous weavers drives my desire to learn about traditional designs and techniques. I strive to understand indigenous cultural symbols and stories and their significance to avoid accidental misappropriation of cultural elements. The patterns in this book do not copy any traditional indigenous motifs out of respect for the rich Diné textile culture.

Churro Sheep

The traditional yarn in southwestern weaving is made from the fleece of Navajo Churro sheep, sometimes called the Original or Old-Style Churro. These desert sheep thrive on sagebrush, shrubs, grasses, and cacti and adapt to seasonal changes like drought. They have excellent mothering instincts and lamb out on the range with little assistance. Churro sheep have a long staple topcoat and a soft undercoat that protects them from the harsh desert and mountain climate of the southwestern US. The fleece is washed, traditionally with yucca root soap, before being naturally dyed using some of the same plants that the Churro sheep eat, including rabbitbrush, piñon, walnut, and oak.

Navajo Shepherding Today

US government action in the 1930s nearly eradicated Navajo Churro sheep, but the efforts of the Diné people, the Navajo Sheep Project, Navajo-Churro Sheep Association, Diné be' iiná (The Navajo Lifeway), and other groups have brought this traditional breed back to the people. Sheep continue to be important in Diné philosophy and culture today, symbolizing living in harmony and balance on the land.

Joe and Carol Benally, of the Dibe' be' iina (Sheep is Life) Ranch on the Navajo Nation in Pinon, Arizona maintain the tradition of Diné shepherding. Joe tells the traditional Navajo history of the sheep:

"These sheep have been in the family since the 1900s and my heritage, culture, language, and food supply depend on the dibe (sheep). It is a way of life, called Dibe' be' iina.

The spirit of the sheep has always been with us. The sheep have always been here including the wild mountain sheep and mountain goat. Navajos already knew about sheep and what they provided. They may have been extinct, but it was told they would reappear. This information was passed down through generations. Just like new discoveries have found that the horse has always been here by finding fossilized remains in this country.

My grandfather was a young child in 1868 during the Long Walk and had sheep way back then in Pinon. They already had sheep and knew how to care for them. Sheep are a traditional part of songs and prayers in the Navajo culture and way of life."

Joe Benally

Indigenous-Made Yarn

Projects in this collection made from the Dibe' be' iina (Sheep is Life) Ranch Navajo Churro yarn include the Valley of Dreams Blanket, the Land of Enchantment Blanket & Pillows, the La Plata Pillow, and the Bears Ears Fringed Pillow. The yarn is undyed, allowing the beauty of the natural colors of the sheep to shine.

The Four Corners collective is another group keeping traditional southwestern and Diné fiber arts alive. Founded in 2018 with the mission of supporting rural and indigenous artists and shepherds in the Four Corners region, this collective pays fair market prices to Diné shepherds and fair wages to hand spinners. The result is gorgeous yarn from Navajo Churro wool from shepherds on the Navajo Nation in Arizona and merino wool from minority-owned Cactus Hill Farm in La Jara, Colorado. Their naturally colored High Desert Heathered yarn is featured in the Modern Bohemian Blanket and Lone Mesa Tote.

Spanish Weaving Traditions

Spanish settlers came to New Mexico in 1540 and their descendants have their own rich weaving tradition. The iconic Spanish weaving style in the southwest is the Rio Grande blanket, woven in two long pieces using a treadle loom then stitched together. These simple striped textiles were the precursor to the Chimayo weaving tradition that continues in northern New Mexico today. They are also the inspiration for the Rio Grande Stripe Towels in this book.

The Spanish-style weaving tradition is carried on by several communities throughout New Mexico. The Trujillo family have been weaving in Chimayo, New Mexico for eight generations. Some of the weaving designs you can find at their Centinela Traditional Arts center include Rio Grande Stripes, Saltillo, Vallero, and Chimayo styles.

Tierra Wools in Chama, New Mexico is another community that is teaching traditional Rio Grande weaving styles and techniques to a new generation of weavers. Their peaceful flock of Churro sheep roam the meadows of the beautiful Chama valley and the Carson National Forest before their fleece is spun into yarn and hand-dyed in a rainbow of colors. Tierra Wools Shepherd's Lamb Churro yarn is used in the Lone Mesa Pillows in this collection.

"Our ancestors came to this valley nearly 200 years ago seeking pasture for their sheep. These hearty souls lived off the land, surviving harsh mountain isolation through cooperation and self-reliance. These values created Tierra Wools. Weaving, wool growing, and shepherding continue as a way of life in the valley, and over the years cooperative breeding programs worked to save the old Spanish Churro sheep line from extinction. The artisans at Tierra Wools are the living link between these generations."

Tierra Wools

Fiber Festivals

Like the sheep shearing and wool sorting gatherings that have occurred each spring for hundreds of years, the fiber festivals of the Four Corners area continue to bring fiber and textile artists together in celebration and collaboration. The two largest local festivals are the Flag Wool & Fiber Festival—held annually on the weekend after Memorial Day in Flagstaff, Arizona—and the Mountain and Valley Wool Festival in Santa Fe, New Mexico—held each fall when the aspens turn golden. These gatherings allow for connection and sharing that will help the traditions of southwestern fiber arts to flourish for generations to come.

One of the things I admire about the traditional pastoral way of shepherding, yarn-making, and weaving in the southwest is that it is deeply connected to the land and in tune with the natural cycle of the seasons. It is a peaceful way of life that honors the wisdom of our ancestors and the natural world. This closeness to the Earth is something I strive for in my daily life as well as my creative work. The original projects in this book use natural wool and cotton yarns produced by local and indigenous shepherds whenever possible to honor this history and promote a sustainable future.

TOOLS & MATERIALS

One thing I love about the art of crochet is that it requires only a hook, a ball of yarn, and imagination to create something beautiful that can last for generations. I keep my crochet hooks in coffee mugs on my bookshelves, where tarnished antique hooks from my grandmothers and old hand-carved wooden hooks mingle with bright, modern, ergonomic hooks. When I begin a project, my first step is to choose a basket or tray to hold the yarn and tools while I crochet. I prefer to use a flat tray for colorwork projects so I can keep the balls of yarn organized in front of me as I crochet. For projects that I travel with, I prefer to use a deeper basket to keep the yarn and tools safe and sound.

Hooks

Ergonomic hooks are helpful to create even stitches and save your hands and wrists from aches and pains. Clover brand hooks are my favorite.

Pillow Forms and Stuffing

Pillow forms create nice plump pillows that last longer than those stuffed with loose polyfill fiber. Polyfill or cotton stuffing is great for unusual shapes like the Sedona Knot Cushion. Pillow forms should be 1–2in (2.5–5cm) larger than the pillow cover on all sides to create a full, even pillow. My favorite brand of pillow forms is ComfyDown, available on Amazon.

Blocking Mats and Pins

Blocking gives your projects a clean, professional look. It can help smooth uneven edges and even out irregular stitches. Foam play mats are my favorite surface to block my projects on. You can also use a carpeted floor, a bed, or several layers of old towels on the floor as a blocking space if you don't own any foam mats. Use blocking combs like Knitter's Pride Knit Blockers or any rust-proof pins to secure your crocheted piece to the surface while it dries.

Yarn

Natural fiber yarns like cotton and wool have the advantages of being breathable, comfortable, and compostable at the end of their life span. The projects in this book use cotton, wool, and linen yarns, but feel free to substitute any synthetic yarns like acrylic of the same weight.

Tapestry Needle

Keep a tapestry needle handy for weaving in yarn ends. To weave in ends of super bulky yarn, a small crochet hook works better than a tapestry needle. I like to store my tapestry needle in a wine cork so it's easy to find in my work basket.

Scissors

Very sharp scissors are a must for trimming fringe neatly.

Measuring Tape

A measuring tape or ruler is useful for checking your gauge, measuring lengths of yarn for tassels or fringe, and for blocking a project into an even rectangle or square.

Highlighter Tape or Washi Tape

To keep track of your progress on a project, place a small piece of highlighter tape, washi tape, or other colored tape on the page just below the row you are working. The tape can be moved down after completing each row.

SIMPLE STITCHES

I love crochet because it is a peaceful, creative, and productive way to spend my time. The repetition of stitches and the soothing flow of yarn through my fingers calms body and mind. The art of creation, freedom of expression, the beauty of color... what's not to love? The projects in this section use only chain, single crochet, half double crochet, or double crochet in easy repeats. They are good choices for when you want to crochet without having to refer to pattern instructions for every row, or when you want to chat while you crochet. Once you get started, you can go with the flow until the last row.

The Rio Grande Stripe Towels are the pretty and practical home décor project you never knew you needed. You will use these absorbent, eco-friendly cotton towels for years. Choose colors to match your kitchen or bathroom for a beautifully coordinated look.

Baskets are my favorite way to store yarn and works in progress. The Artisan Market Baskets are a great way to use up odd balls of yarn and they will fly off your display table if you sell your work. I was surprised by how popular they were the first time I brought a batch to our local artisan market.

We often crochet gifts for others, but the Cozy Yogi Wrap is a wonderful gift to make for yourself. Of all the wearable crochet items I have made, I appreciate this one the most. On long road trips it keeps me cozy in the passenger seat while my husband drives. It's easily packable and less bulky than a blanket, warm and breathable in light moss stitch lace.

Pillows and cushions are among my favorite projects because I can often make one in a weekend. The Sedona Knot Cushion has a unique construction; it's a long tube that is tied in a knot after it is crocheted and stuffed. Have some fun and create something out of the ordinary that is especially beloved by kids and teens.

The Modern Bohemian Blanket is the largest project in this section, but it's an easy one to travel with because it is made from 13 smaller pieces. You can customize the pattern to make any size blanket by adding more rounds or skipping the last few rounds of each piece.

RIO GRANDE
Stripe Towels

The snowy San Juan mountains in Colorado where I live are the source of the Rio Grande river, which winds its way down to the sunny Gulf of Mexico. My little town of Bayfield, Colorado has only one traffic light and is surrounded by mountains, ranches, national forests, and the Southern Ute and Navajo tribal lands. You can still see the old west around town in the buildings and in the traditions of the people who choose to live so far from the nearest interstate highway.

San Juan Mountains, Colorado

Yarn colors from left to right: Bamboo, Coral Rose, Tea Rose, Tangerine, Pretty in Pink, Wine, Overcast, Sage, Jade Mist, Mod Blue, Teal, and Dark Pine.

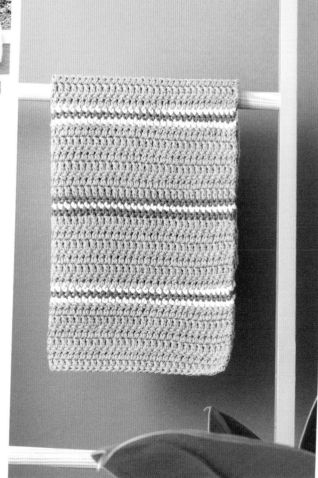

The Rio Grande weaving tradition of New Mexico inspired this pattern. Woven Rio Grande blankets typically have five, seven, or nine stripes. Simple Rio Grande blankets with a predominant background color are sometimes called *fresada del campo* or camp blankets. More elaborate blankets are often given as wedding gifts, with the outer sets of stripes representing the bride and groom individually and the center stripes representing their newly formed family. Here, the classic cotton towel gets a modern update for the kitchen or bathroom. Use cotton, bamboo, hemp, or linen yarn for maximum absorbency for drying hands or dishes, cleaning countertops, walls, or floors, or for baby burp cloths or diaper changing mats. This easy pattern uses only single and double crochet stitches, in a relaxing repeat of six rows of double crochet followed by three rows of single crochet. I bet you can't stop after making just one!

SUPPLIES

YARN

Worsted (aran) weight in three colors

Main Color (MC): 285yd (261m)

Contrast Color 1 (CC1): 40yd (37m)

Contrast Color 2 (CC2): 40yd (37m)

Shown in Lily Sugar 'n Cream yarn (100% cotton); 120yd (110m)/70.9g: Ecru (CC1) and Warm Brown (CC2), MC colors: Wine, Pretty in Pink, Tangerine, Tea Rose, Coral Rose, Bamboo, Overcast, Sage, Dark Pine, Teal, Mod Blue, and Jade Mist

HOOK

4mm (G/6) crochet hook

GAUGE

14 sts and 8 rows = 4in (10cm) in dc

SIZE

17 x 21in (43 x 53cm)

Pattern Notes

To keep the edges straight, count your stitches after the first few rows. It's easy to lose the very last double crochet stitch of each row, which is worked into the starting chain of the previous row. To change colors, finish the last stitch of the row by yarning over with the new color. You can crochet over the ends to secure them. Lay the ends along the top edge of your work. Catch the old color yarn tail and the new yarn tail inside the first five or six stitches.

TOWEL

Ch 62.

Row 1: Dc in 3rd ch from hook and all ch across, turn. (60 dc)

Rows 2–6: Ch 3 (counts as a dc), 59 dc, turn. (60 dc)

Fasten off MC.

Row 7: Using CC1, ch 1 (does not count as st), 60 sc, turn. (60 sc)

Row 8: Using CC2, rep Row 7.

Row 9: Using CC1, rep Row 7.

Rows 10–15: Using MC, rep Row 2.

Row 16: Using CC2, rep Row 7.

Row 17: Using CC1, rep Row 7.

Row 18: Using CC2, rep Row 7.

Rows 19–24: Using MC, rep Row 2.

Rows 25–27: Rep Rows 7–9.

Rows 28–33: Using MC, rep Row 2.

Rows 34–36: Rep Rows 16–18.

Rows 37–42: Using MC, rep Row 2.

Rows 43–45: Rep Rows 7–9.

Rows 46–51: Using MC, rep Row 2.

Fasten off.

Finishing

Weave in ends.

Block to dimensions if desired.

ARTISAN MARKET
Baskets

These boutique-worthy baskets made from scrap yarn are best sellers at the outdoor artisan market hosted by the Billy Goat Saloon in my little mountain town every summer. They make perfect gifts for friends and family, or a thoughtful house-warming gift with a plant inside. Excellent for storing hats, gloves, mittens, scarves... and yarn, of course!

This is a use-what-you've-got project for when you find yourself with a lot of odds and ends of yarn. Crochet with seven strands of yarn held together as if they were one. Mixing yarns of different weights and textures gives the basket a lovely tweedy look. Make something pretty and practical while you make room for new yarn purchases! You can use up very short yarn scraps and tie knots to join a new strand of yarn. Leave tails of at least 3in (8cm) at each knot. The knots will be hidden inside the basket. You can crochet over the yarn tails from each knot to help secure them.

Choose shorter handles for a storage basket or longer straps to carry the basket as a tote. Because the basket is made with seven strands of yarn at once, it makes a very sturdy tote for carrying heavy items like glass bottles. You can repurpose an old belt for the handles. I like to join the handles using screw-in rivets, also known as Chicago screws. You can also attach handles by sewing them to the basket with yarn and a tapestry needle.

SUPPLIES

YARN
Any yarns from fingering to bulky (chunky) weight, about 1¼lb (550g) of mixed yarn scraps for a small basket or 2¼lb (1kg) of mixed yarn scraps for a large basket

OTHER MATERIALS
¾in (2cm)-wide leather or faux leather strap: 18–20in (46–51cm) per basket for short handles or 60in (152cm) per basket for long straps, 8 screw-in rivets (Chicago screws) per basket (optional)

HOOK
8mm (L/11) crochet hook

GAUGE
9 rounds = 4in (10cm) in sc

SIZE
Small: 12in wide x 10in tall (30.5cm wide x 25.5cm tall)

Large: 15in wide x 12in tall (38cm wide x 30.5cm tall)

The basket is worked in a continuous spiral without joining between rounds. The work is not turned after each round; the right side is kept facing up throughout. The sides of the basket are worked in a continuous spiral from the round bottom base.

BASKET

Round Bottom
Ch 2.

Round 1: 8 sc in 2nd ch from hook. (8 sc)

Round 2: 2 sc in each st. (16 sc)

Round 3: [2 sc in next st, 1 sc in next st] 8 times. (24 sc)

Round 4: [2 sc in next st, 1 sc in next 2 sts] 8 times. (32 sc)

Round 5: [2 sc in next st, 1 sc in next 3 sts] 8 times. (40 sc)

Round 6: [2 sc in next st, 1 sc in next 4 sts] 8 times. (48 sc)

Round 7: [2 sc in next st, 1 sc in next 5 sts] 8 times. (56 sc)

Round 8: Sc in each st. (56 sc)

Round 9: [2 sc in next st, 1 sc in next 6 sts] 8 times. (64 sc)

Round 10: Sc in each st. (64 sc)

Small Size

Skip to Sides.

Large Size

Continue to Round 11.

Round 11: [2 sc in next st, 1 sc in next 7 sts] 8 times. (72 sc)

Round 12: Sc in each st. (72 sc)

Round 13: [2 sc in next st, 1 sc in next 8 sts] 8 times. (80 sc)

Round 14: Sc in each st. (80 sc)

Round 15: [2 sc in next st, 1 sc in next 9 sts] 8 times. (88 sc)

Round 16: Sc in each st. (88 sc)

Continue to Sides without fastening off.

Sides

Round 1: Sc in BLO of each st. (64 sc for Small or 88 sc for Large)

Rounds 2–16: Sc through both loops of each st.

Small Size

Fasten off.

Large Size

Continue to Round 17.

Rounds 17–21: Sc through both loops of each st.

Fasten off and weave in ends.

Finishing
Cut two 9in (23cm) pieces of strap for a small basket, two 10in (25.5cm) pieces of strap for a large basket, or two 30in (76cm) pieces of strap for a tote with shoulder straps. Punch two or four holes in the end of each strap piece using a hole punch, skewer, awl, or pocketknife. Attach the strap to the basket or tote using screw-in rivets or sew it to the basket with yarn and a needle.

COZY YOGI
Wrap

The Cozy Yogi Wrap is an oversized rectangle that blurs the line between wrap and yoga blanket. It was inspired by my evening walk home from yoga class at our neighborhood community center. The trail curves around a small lake, where I love to watch wild beavers glide out from their lodge for a sunset swim. I use the wrap to keep cozy as I relax in *savasana* pose at the end of my yoga practice. Then it keeps me blissfully warm on my walk home so I can linger under the twinkling stars a few minutes longer.

When the sun goes down, the stars come out for a breathtaking view of the Milky Way on my walk home. The remoteness of our neighborhood in the forests of southwest Colorado, hours from any big city lights, creates spectacular conditions for stargazing. The town motto here in Bayfield is "Where Stars Shine Bright" for good reason.

This wrap combines my love for traveling light with my desire to have a yoga blanket during and after class. It's pretty and practical and pairs as well with yoga pants and a messy bun as it does with tall leather boots and jeans for sipping apple cider at the fall harvest festivals. Take it along on a hike to keep you warm and use it as a picnic blanket too!

SUPPLIES

YARN
Fingering weight or fine weight in two colors

Main Color (MC): 730yd (668m)

Contrast Color (CC): 730yd (668m)

Shown in Freia Fibers Fingering Shawl Ball; 430yd (393m)/100g; Dusk (MC, 2 balls) and Elephant (CC, 2 balls)

HOOK
6mm (J/10) crochet hook)

GAUGE
17 sts and 16 rows = 4in (10cm) in pattern after wet blocking

SIZE
32 x 72in (81 x 183cm) in pattern after wet blocking

Pattern Notes

Self-striping or ombré gradient yarn is the main color (MC). A solid color yarn is the contrast color (CC). When changing from MC to CC or vice versa, attach the new yarn to the first stitch of the row with a slip stitch. For a symmetrical wrap using gradient yarn cakes, begin using the second cake of MC yarn at Row 144 for the second half of the wrap; control color changes if necessary to mirror the first half of the wrap. For Rows 3–264, the last stitch of each row is worked into the top of the ch-2 that started the previous row. To make a wrap with DK weight yarn, use a 6.5mm (K/10½) hook and omit Rows 133–143.

WRAP

Using MC, ch 130.

Row 1: Sc in 2nd ch from hook and all ch across, turn. (129 sts)

Row 2: Ch 2 (counts as first sc and ch 1 throughout), sc in 3rd st from hook, [ch 1, skip next st, sc in next st] 64 times, turn. (129 sts)

Row 3: Ch 2, [sc in ch-1 space, ch 1] 63 times, skip last ch-1 space, 1 sc in last st, turn.

Rows 4–11: Rep Row 3.

Fasten off MC.

Row 12: Attach CC yarn with a sl st into first st of previous row, rep Row 3.

Fasten off.

Rows 13–22: Using MC yarn, rep Row 3. (10 rows MC)

Rows 23 and 24: Using CC yarn, rep Row 3. (2 rows CC)

Rows 25–33: Using MC yarn, rep Row 3. (9 rows MC)

Rows 34–36: Using CC yarn, rep Row 3. (3 rows CC)

Rows 37–44: Using MC yarn, rep Row 3. (8 rows MC)

Rows 45–48: Using CC yarn, rep Row 3. (4 rows CC)

Rows 49–55: Using MC yarn, rep Row 3. (7 rows MC)

Rows 56–60: Using CC yarn, rep Row 3. (5 rows CC)

Rows 61–66: Using MC yarn, rep Row 3. (6 rows MC)

Rows 67–72: Using CC yarn, rep Row 3. (6 rows CC)

Rows 73–77: Using MC yarn, rep Row 3. (5 rows MC)

Rows 78–84: Using CC yarn, rep Row 3. (7 rows CC)

Rows 85–88: Using MC yarn, rep Row 3. (4 rows MC)

Rows 89–96: Using CC yarn, rep Row 3. (8 rows CC)

Rows 97–99: Using MC yarn, rep Row 3. (3 rows MC)

Rows 100–108: Using CC yarn, rep Row 3. (9 rows CC)

Rows 109 and 110: Using MC yarn, rep Row 3. (2 rows MC)

Rows 111–120: Using CC yarn, rep Row 3. (10 rows CC)

Row 121: Using MC yarn, rep Row 3. (1 row MC)

Rows 122–143: Using CC yarn, rep Row 3. (22 rows CC)

Row 144: Using MC yarn, rep Row 3. (1 row MC)

Rows 145–154: Using CC yarn, rep Row 3. (10 rows CC)

Rows 155 and 156: Using MC yarn, rep Row 3. (2 rows MC)

Rows 157–165: Using CC yarn, rep Row 3. (9 rows CC)

Rows 166–168: Using MC yarn, rep Row 3. (3 rows MC)

Rows 169–176: Using CC yarn, rep Row 3. (8 rows CC)

Rows 177–180: Using MC yarn, rep Row 3. (4 rows MC)

Rows 181–187: Using CC yarn, rep Row 3. (7 rows CC)

Rows 188–192: Using MC yarn, rep Row 3. (5 rows MC)

Rows 193–198: Using CC yarn, rep Row 3. (6 rows CC)

Rows 199–204: Using MC yarn, rep Row 3. (6 rows MC)

Rows 205–209: Using CC yarn, rep Row 3. (5 rows CC)

Rows 210–216: Using MC yarn, rep Row 3. (7 rows MC)

Rows 217–220: Using CC yarn, rep Row 3. (4 rows CC)

Rows 221–228: Using MC yarn, rep Row 3. (8 rows MC)

Rows 229–231: Using CC yarn, rep Row 3. (3 rows CC)

Rows 232–240: Using MC yarn, rep Row 3. (9 rows MC)

Rows 241 and 242: Using CC yarn, rep Row 3. (2 rows CC)

Rows 243–252: Using MC yarn, rep Row 3. (10 rows MC)

Row 253: Using CC yarn, rep Row 3. (1 row CC)

Rows 254–264: Using MC yarn, rep Row 3. (11 rows MC)

Fasten off.

Finishing

Weave in all ends.

Block to dimensions if desired.

MODERN BOHEMIAN
Blanket

This fringed blanket has a soothing geometric diamond design. Diamonds are a common motif in European, Middle Eastern, and Asian textiles as well as in the southwest. In the Navajo, Apache, and Hopi traditions, the diamond symbolizes the four winds, the four elements of earth, fire, air, and water, freedom, eternity, unity, and balance. The four points also represent the Four Corners of the *Dinétah* or Navajo homeland, with each corner marked by a sacred mountain. In Anatolian kilim weaving, a diamond pattern represents the eye. This motif creates an amulet of protection from the evil eye and provides good luck for the weaver and their family.

Further east in Indonesia, triangles along the borders of a cloth represent the protective teeth of a guardian deity. Empower your blanket with the symbolism of these textile motifs or just enjoy the meditative rhythm of each round as you stitch. In this unique variation of Pretty Peaceful's classic Modern Bohemian Blanket pattern, it's easy to play with color combinations to suit your style or to use scrap yarn. A boho macramé fringe turns your blanket into a magic carpet!

SUPPLIES

YARN

Worsted (aran) weight, 4,800yd (4,389m) plus 880yd (805m) for the border and fringe

Shown in Four Corners Yarns High Desert Heathered (50% Navajo Churro wool, 50% merino wool); 200yd (183m)/105g: Magenta Berry (1 skein), Smokey Lavender (1 skein), Brick (1 skein), Rust (1 skein), Mustard (1 skein), Goldenseal (1 skein), Olive (1 skein), Fern (1 skein), Aqua (1 skein), Dragonfly (1 skein), Undyed Gray (2 skeins), Pink (2 skeins), Teal (2 skeins), Aloe (2 skeins), Soft Sage (2 skeins), and Violet (2 skeins), plus 4 more skeins of Rust for the border and macramé fringe (optional)

YARN ALTERNATIVES

Patons Classic Wool Worsted, Brown Sheep Lamb's Pride Worsted, Cascade 220, Knit Picks Wool of the Andes Worsted, Stylecraft Special Aran, Lily Sugar 'n Cream cotton

HOOK

5mm (H/8) crochet hook

GAUGE

8 rounds = 4in (10cm)

SIZE

57 x 78in (145 x 198cm)

Pattern Notes

This blanket is crocheted in 13 pieces, each worked in the round. The pieces are one center diamond, two blunted diamonds, two end triangles, and eight side triangles. Each of these pieces is composed of blocks of five double crochet stitches worked in rounds (center and blunted diamonds) or half-rounds (end and side triangles). You can adjust the size of your blanket by adding or subtracting rounds from each of the 13 pieces. The side triangles must have one less round than the other pieces so they fit together properly. Fasten off after each round. Change colors after every two rounds. The pieces are sewn together with a mattress stitch. To create an invisible seam, use the same color of yarn for the last round of each of the 13 pieces. The starting ch-3 counts as a dc stitch.

A

B

C

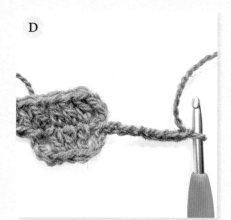

D

BLANKET

Center Diamond

(make 1)

Round 1: Ch 7, dc in 4th ch from hook, dc in next 3 ch (1 block of 5 dc made) (A), turn work clockwise 180º, keeping the RS of the work facing up.

Round 2: Ch 7, dc in 4th ch from hook, dc in next 3 ch (B), sl st to the top of the starting ch from Round 1, ch 3, 3 dc, ch 3, sl st to next st (C), turn work clockwise 180º, ch 7 (D), dc in 4th ch from hook, dc in next 3 ch, sl st to top of first dc (E), ch 3, 3 dc, ch 3, sl st to next st (F). (4 blocks of 5 dc made)

Fasten off.

Round 3: Attach yarn to lower right corner of the right-most block (G), ch 7, dc in 4th ch from hook, dc in next 3 ch, sl st to first st at top of block, ch 3, 4 dc, sl st to next st, ch 3, 3 dc, ch 3, sl st to next st, 4 dc, ch 3, sl st to next st (H), turn work clockwise 180º, ch 7 (I), dc in 4th ch from hook, dc in next 3 ch, sl st to top of first dc, ch 3, 4 dc, sl st to next st, ch 3, 3 dc, ch 3, sl st to next st, 4 dc, ch 3, sl st to next st. (8 blocks of 5 dc made)

Fasten off.

Round 4: Attach yarn to lower right corner of the right-most block, *ch 7 (J), dc in 4th ch from hook, dc in next 3 ch, sl st to first st at top of block, [ch 3, 4 dc, sl st to next st] twice**, ch 3, 3 dc, ch 3, sl st to next st, [4 dc, ch 3, sl st to next st] twice***, turn work clockwise 180º, rep from *. (12 blocks of 5 dc made)

Fasten off.

Rounds 5–17: Rep Round 4 adding a rep of [ch 3, 4 dc, sl st to next st] at the ** and a rep of [4 dc, ch 3, sl st to next st] at the *** in each round. (64 blocks of 5 dc made after Round 17)

Fasten off.

E
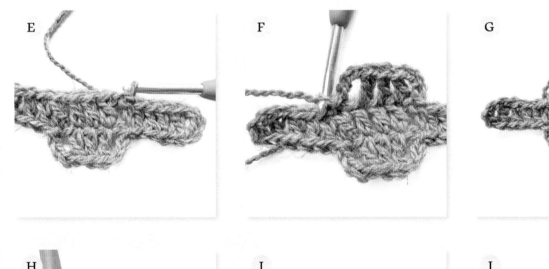

F

G

H

I

J
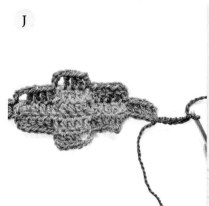

Blunted Diamond

(make 2)

Rounds 1–16: Work as for Center Diamond.

Round 17: Attach yarn to lower right corner of the right-most block, ch 7, dc in 4th ch from hook, dc in next 3 ch, sl st to first st at top of block, *[ch 3, 4 dc, sl st to next st] 15 times, fasten off without creating a block at the top of the diamond (K), skip next 4 sts, reattach yarn to next st with a sl st, [4 dc, ch 3, sl st to next st] 15 times, turn work clockwise 180°, ch 7, dc in 4th ch from hook, dc in next 3 ch, sl st to top of first dc, rep from *. (62 blocks of 5 dc made)

Fasten off.

End Triangle

(make 2)

Round 1: Ch 7, dc in 4th ch from hook, dc in next 3 ch, turn work clockwise 180°. (1 block of 5 dc made)

Round 2: Ch 7, dc in 4th ch from hook, dc in next 3 ch, sl st to first st at top of block (into the top of the last dc of Round 1), ch 3, 3 dc, ch 3, sl st to next st, turn work clockwise 180°, ch 7, dc in 4th ch from hook, dc in next 3 ch, sl st to top of first dc. (3 blocks of 5 dc made) (L)

Fasten off.

Round 3: Attach yarn to lower right corner of the right-most block, ch 7 (M), dc in 4th ch from hook, dc in next 3 ch, sl st to first st at top of block (N), ch 3, 4 dc, sl st to next st, ch 3, 3 dc, ch 3, sl st to next st, 4 dc, ch 3, sl st to next st, turn work clockwise 180°, ch 7 (O), dc in 4th ch from hook, dc in next 3 ch, sl st to top of first dc. (5 blocks of 5 dc made)

Fasten off.

Round 4: Attach yarn to lower right corner of the right-most block (P), ch 7, dc in 4th ch from hook, dc in next 3 ch, sl st to first st at top of block, [ch 3, 4 dc, sl st to next st] twice*, ch 3, 3 dc, ch 3, sl st to next st, [4 dc, ch 3, sl st to next st] twice**, turn work clockwise 180°, ch 7, dc in 4th ch from hook, dc in next 3 ch, sl st to top of first dc. (7 blocks of 5 dc made)

Fasten off.

Rounds 5–17: Repeat Round 4, adding a rep of [ch 3, 4 dc, sl st to next st] at the * and a rep of [4 dc, ch 3, sl st to next st] at the ** in each round. (33 blocks of 5 dc made after Round 17)

Fasten off.

K

L

M

N

O

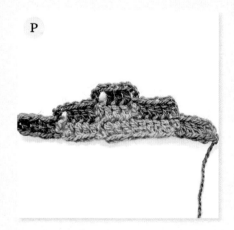

P

Side Triangle

(make 8)

Round 1: Ch 7, dc in 4th ch from hook, dc in next 3 ch. (1 block of 5 dc made) (Q)

Fasten off.

Round 2: Attach yarn to the first dc at the upper right corner of block, ch 3, 3 dc, ch 3, sl st to next st (R), turn work clockwise 180º, ch 7, dc in 4th ch from hook, dc in next 3 ch (S), sl st to first st at top of block, ch 3, 4 dc. (3 blocks of 5 dc made)

Fasten off.

Round 3: Attach yarn to the first dc at the upper right corner of the first block of Round 2, ch 3 (T), 3 dc, ch 3, sl st to next st, 4 dc, ch 3, sl st to next st, turn work clockwise 180º, ch 7 (U), dc in 4th ch from hook, dc in next 3 ch, sl st to first st at top of block, [ch 3, 4 dc, sl st to next st] twice. (5 blocks of 5 dc made)

Fasten off.

Round 4: Attach yarn to the first dc at the upper right corner of first block of Round 3, ch 3 (V), 3 dc, ch 3, sl st to next st, [4 dc, ch 3, sl st to next st] twice*, turn work clockwise 180º, ch 7, dc in 4th ch from hook, dc in next 3 ch, sl st to first st at top of block, [ch 3, 4 dc, sl st to next st] twice**, ch 3, 4 dc. (7 blocks of 5 dc made)

Fasten off.

Rounds 5–16: Rep Round 4, adding a rep of [4 dc, ch 3, sl st to next st] at the * and a rep of [ch 3, 4 dc, sl st to next st] at the ** in each round. (31 blocks of 5 dc made after Round 16)

Fasten off.

Q

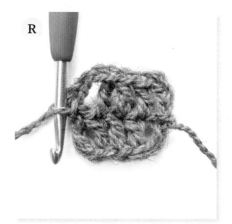

R

S

T

U

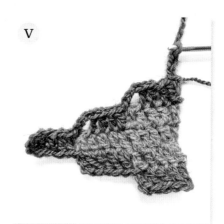

V

Finishing

Using the same color yarn as the last round of each section, sew the pieces together using the mattress stitch. Line up the double crochet stitches of the blocks and sew, picking up one loop by inserting the needle into the back of the work and pulling through to the front (W). Then insert the needle from the back of the work through one loop of the matching stitch on the opposite piece to the front of the work (X). Stitch into the place where the slip stitch at the inner corner of one block meets the chain at the outer corner of the other block to secure them before moving on to the next block (Y).

Weave in all ends.

Border

Attach yarn to one short end of the blanket, two or three stitches from the corner.

Round 1: Ch 1, sc evenly around blanket, working 3 sc in each corner and 2 sc into each dc along the long edges, sl st to first sc.

Rounds 2–7: Sc in each sc, working 3 sc in each corner st, sl st to first sc.

Fasten off and weave in ends. Block if desired.

Fringe

Cut 516 pieces of yarn 18in (46cm) long in the same color yarn as the border. Each cluster of fringe contains six pieces of yarn except the fringes on each end which contain three pieces of yarn each. Starting at a corner of the short end of the blanket, insert a hook into the corner stitch from the back of the work to the front, fold three pieces of yarn in half, grab the center with the hook and pull through about 2in (5cm), tuck the yarn ends through the loop and tighten the knot. *Skip the next three stitches, insert the hook into the next stitch from the back of the work to the front, fold six pieces of yarn in half, grab the center with the hook and pull through about 2in (5cm), tuck the yarn ends through the loop and tighten the knot. Repeat from * across the blanket. For the last cluster of fringes, use only three pieces of yarn.

Macramé Fringe (Optional):

Starting at the right-hand side of the blanket, tie all six strands of the end fringe with six strands from the next fringe to the left in a square knot about 1in (2.5cm) below the blanket edge. Pull the knot tight. Rep with the next fringe, tying the remaining six strands of the right-most fringe in a knot with six strands from the next fringe to the left. Repeat across the blanket on both ends.

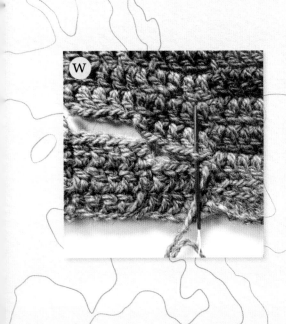

Charts

Each cell represents one block of five double crochet stitches.

Work from the center out in rounds or half rounds.

Center Diamond

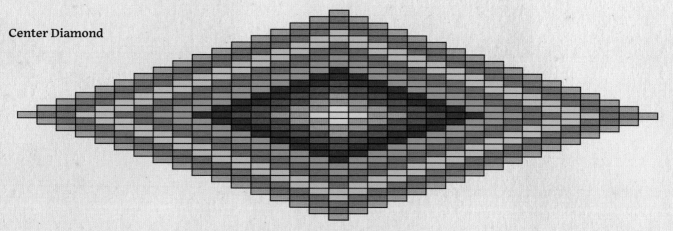

Blunted Diamond

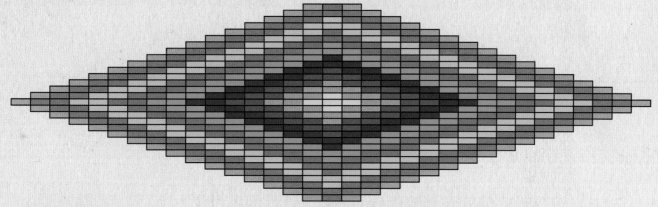

End Triangle

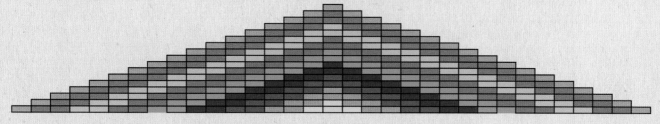

Side Triangle

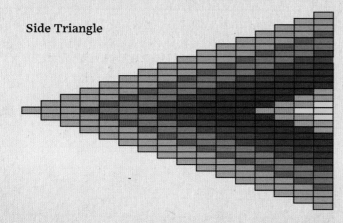

SEDONA
Knot Cushion

Sedona, Arizona is a mecca for spiritual seekers drawn to its beautiful red sandstone rock formations and famous "energy vortexes," which are said to support healing, meditation, and self-exploration. The Sedona Knot Cushion is a yoga or meditation cushion for peaceful mornings and mindful moments. Sit in silence outdoors to clear your mind and find peace within. Or rest your head for an afternoon nap and wake up enlightened! Knots are symbolic of love, connection, and infinity. This simple knot cushion is relaxing to crochet and fun to tie.

You can find vortexes throughout Sedona's mesas and canyons, but my favorite is Buddha Beach in Crescent Moon State Park. The soft orange canyon walls create a gorgeous contrast silhouetted against bright azure skies. The canyon cradles the clear, babbling Oak Creek, which provides a sweet cool breeze among the juniper and oak trees. It's an oasis in the dry, dusty Arizona chaparral, a beautiful place to meditate or reconnect with the healing power of nature.

SUPPLIES

YARN
Bulky (chunky) weight, 2,880yd
(2,634m)

Shown in Knit Picks Billow
(100% cotton); 120yd
(110m)/100g: Natural Billow
(24 skeins)

YARN ALTERNATIVES
Red Heart Super Saver,
Stylecraft Special Aran, Cygnet
Boho Spirit

OTHER MATERIALS
Polyfill toy stuffing

HOOK
6.5mm (K/10½) crochet hook

GAUGE
10 sts and 8 rows = 4in (10cm)
in hdc

SIZE
Tube: 11ft (335cm) long x 9½in
(24cm) circumference

Cushion: about 18in (46cm)
diameter x 9in (23cm) tall

Pattern Notes

This pattern is worked in the amigurumi style, in a spiral without slip stitching or turning chains. Crochet with three strands of yarn held together as one. The long, hollow tube is filled with polyfill stuffing, then tied in an overhand knot, and finally the ends of the tube are secured around the free loop and sewn together. Stuff the tube as you go, adding a handful of polyfill every ten rounds or so. The tube should be stuffed quite firmly for a seat cushion to about 9½in (24cm) in diameter—stuff it more loosely for use as a pillow.

Mattress stitch: *insert threaded needle from the back of the work up through the front loop only of a stitch on one tube end, then insert the needle from the back of the work up through the front loop only of a matching stitch on the other tube end; rep from * around.

TUBE

Ch 24, join with sl st in first ch to form a ring.

Round 1: Hdc around. (24 sts)

Rounds 2–323: Rep Round 1.

Fasten off, leaving an 18in (46cm) tail for sewing seam.

Finishing

Fold the tube in half. Tie the doubled tube in an overhand knot (A, B). Pull one tube end through the free loop (C). With a tapestry needle and the yarn tail, join the tube ends around the free loop with mattress stitch (D). Weave in ends.

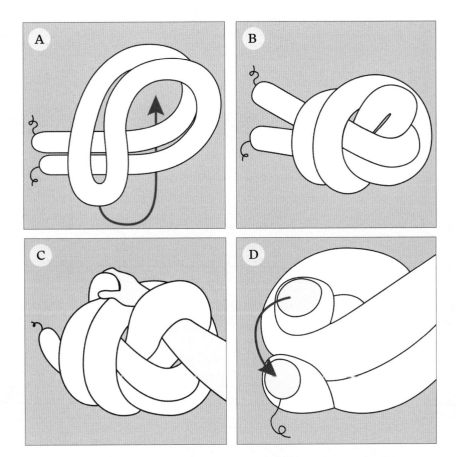

TEXTURED STITCHES

Yarn is a wonderful medium for creative work because of its endless variety of colors and textures. Once we have selected the yarn, we can create infinite variations in textures with just slight changes to our usual single and double crochet stitches. The patterns in this section use gentle color palettes to allow the texture of the yarn and stitches to shine.

The Durango Pillows have a subtle texture created by crocheting through the front loop only of the contrast color stitches. I think the resulting fabric looks like it was woven on a loom. It's a simple, modern way to add a bit of interest to a pillow that fits in with any décor.

Creating a plump, round bobble stitch from smooth, flat yarn is a joyous act. Tiny bobbles are irresistibly squishy and fun. They add a cushy comfort to the La Plata Rug and matching pillows. The Valley of Dreams Blanket brings the marshmallow fun of bobbles together with dainty filet crochet lace. It's an unexpected combination that makes for a striking and unforgettable blanket.

Mosaic crochet creates texture with a beautiful dimension. By alternating rows of single crochet stitches through the back loop only and double crochet stitches through the front loop only, we create a flat, shadowed background that pops the pattern forward in three dimensions. The Dreamer's Path Wrap and the Cactus Garden Blanket share the addictive "just one more row!" quality of overlay mosaic crochet—it's hard to put down.

Perhaps the most luxurious textures in this section are created by simple fringe. A thick layer of fringes on the ends of a rug transforms it into a bohemian masterpiece. The Bears Ears Fringed Pillow creates an irresistibly soft, touchable texture by adding short pieces of fringe onto a simple single crochet background. It's a bold statement that is as fun to make as it is to use in your living room or bedroom.

DURANGO
Pillows

Give your home some modern, minimalist style with this set of pillows inspired by the free-spirited mountain town of Durango, Colorado. Durango is close to the New Mexico border, nestled between the Southern Ute and Ute Mountain reservations. The Animas River flows through the center of town, the glittering crown jewel of the Animas River valley, which is home to towering red rock cliffs, natural hot springs, and endless forests of aspen and pine. In autumn, the aspen leaves turn gold. It's a lovely display of natural beauty against the deep green ponderosa pine and the russet reds and oranges of the Gambel oak shrubs.

The people of Durango are independent, laid-back, and outdoorsy. The city is unique in that you could rock climb, mountain bike, and float the river in one day without leaving town! Southwestern cowboy and vintage boho fashion are alive and well on the streets. It's a town with an appreciation for the arts, home to the historic Toh-Atin Gallery featuring the work of artists from over 20 different tribes.

SUPPLIES

YARN

Worsted (aran) weight

Small: Main Color (MC) 558yd (510m), Contrast Color (CC) 93yd (85m)

Large: Main Color (MC) 840yd (768m), Contrast Color (CC) 160yd (146m)

Shown in Lion Brand Pima Cotton yarn (100% cotton); 186yd (170m)/100g:
Small: 140R Rose Taupe (MC, 3 balls) and 099R Vintage (CC, 1 ball)
Large: 099 Vintage (MC, 5 balls) and 140R Rose Taupe (CC, 1 ball)

OTHER MATERIALS

18in (46cm) and/or 24in (61cm) square pillow form

HOOK

3.75mm (F/5) crochet hook

GAUGE

17 sts and 17 rows = 4in (10cm) in sc

SIZE

Small: 17in (43cm) square to fit an 18in (46cm) square pillow form

Large: 22½in (57cm) square to fit a 24in (61cm) square pillow form

Pattern Notes

In this easy set of pillows, single crochet stitches through the front loop only create a woven-like textile. The yarn can be cut at each color change and yarn tails pulled to the back side of the work and knotted, with the knots hidden inside the finished pillow, so there's no need to carry yarn or weave in the yarn ends. To change colors, yarn over with the new color to complete the last stitch in the old color. The work is turned after every row.

FRONT/BACK FOR SMALL PILLOW

(make 2)

Using MC, ch 69.

Row 1: Sc in 2nd ch from hook and each ch across, turn. (68 sts)

Rows 2–11: Ch 1 (does not count as a st here or throughout), 68 sc MC, turn.

Fasten off MC after Row 11.

Row 12: Using CC, ch 1, 4 sc, 60 sc MC, 4 sc CC, fasten off, turn.

Row 13: Using MC, ch 1, 4 sc in FLO, 60 sc, 4 sc in FLO, fasten off, turn.

Row 14: Using CC, ch 1, 8 sc, 52 sc MC, 8 sc CC, fasten off, turn.

Row 15: Using MC, ch 1, 8 sc in FLO, 52 sc, 8 sc in FLO, fasten off, turn.

Row 16: Using CC, ch 1, 12 sc, 44 sc MC, 12 sc CC, fasten off, turn.

Row 17: Using MC, ch 1, 12 sc in FLO, 44 sc, 12 sc in FLO, fasten off, turn.

Row 18: Using CC, ch 1, 16 sc, 36 sc MC, 16 sc CC, fasten off, turn.

Row 19: Using MC, ch 1, 16 sc in FLO, 36 sc, 16 sc in FLO, fasten off, turn.

Row 20: Using CC, ch 1, 20 sc, 28 sc MC, 20 sc CC, fasten off, turn.

Row 21: Using MC, ch 1, 20 sc in FLO, 28 sc, 20 sc in FLO, fasten off, turn.

Row 22: Using CC, ch 1, 24 sc, 20 sc MC, 24 sc CC, fasten off, turn.

Row 23: Using MC, ch 1, 24 sc in FLO, 20 sc, 24 sc in FLO, fasten off, turn.

Row 24: Rep Row 20.

Row 25: Rep Row 21.

Row 26: Rep Row 18.

Row 27: Rep Row 19.

Row 28: Rep Row 16.

Row 29: Rep Row 17.

Row 30: Rep Row 14.

Row 31: Rep Row 15.

Row 32: Rep Row 12.

Row 33: Rep Row 13.

Rows 34–43: Using MC, ch 1, 68 sc, turn.

Fasten off MC after Row 43.

Rows 44–75: Rep Rows 12–43.

Fasten off.

FRONT/BACK FOR LARGE PILLOW

(make 2)

Using MC, ch 93.

Row 1: 1 sc in 2nd ch from hook and each ch across, turn. (92 sts)

Rows 2–13: Ch 1 (does not count as st here or throughout), 92 sc MC, turn.

Fasten off MC after Row 13.

Row 14: Using CC, ch 1, 4 sc, 84 sc MC, 4 sc CC, fasten off, turn.

Row 15: Using MC, ch 1, 4 sc in FLO, 84 sc, 4 sc in FLO, fasten off, turn.

Row 16: Using CC, ch 1, 8 sc, 76 sc MC, 8 sc CC, fasten off, turn.

Row 17: Using MC, ch 1, 8 sc in FLO, 76 sc, 8 sc in FLO, fasten off, turn.

Row 18: Using CC, ch 1, 12 sc, 68 sc MC, 12 sc CC, fasten off, turn.

Row 19: Using MC, ch 1, 12 sc in FLO, 68 sc, 12 sc in FLO, fasten off, turn.

Row 20: Using CC, ch 1, 16 sc, 60 sc MC, 16 sc CC, fasten off, turn.

Row 21: Using MC, ch 1, 16 sc in FLO, 60 sc, 16 sc in FLO, fasten off, turn.

Row 22: Using CC, ch 1, 20 sc, 52 sc MC, 20 sc CC, fasten off, turn.

Row 23: Using MC, ch 1, 20 sc in FLO, 52 sc, 20 sc in FLO, fasten off, turn.

Row 24: Using CC, ch 1, 24 sc, 44 sc MC, 24 sc CC, fasten off, turn.

Row 25: Using MC, ch 1, 24 sc in FLO, 44 sc, 24 sc in FLO, fasten off, turn.

Row 26: Using CC, ch 1, 28 sc, 36 sc MC, 28 sc CC, fasten off, turn.

Row 27: Using MC, ch 1, 28 sc in FLO, 36 sc, 28 sc in FLO, fasten off, turn.

Row 28: Using CC, ch 1, 32 sc, 28 sc MC, 32 sc CC, fasten off, turn.

Row 29: Using MC, ch 1, 32 sc in FLO, 28 sc, 32 sc in FLO, fasten off, turn.

Row 30: Rep Row 26.

Row 31: Rep Row 27.

Row 32: Rep Row 24.

Row 33: Rep Row 25.

Row 34: Rep Row 22.

Row 35: Rep Row 23.

Row 36: Rep Row 20.

Row 37: Rep Row 21.

Row 38: Rep Row 18.

Row 39: Rep Row 19.

Row 40: Rep Row 16.

Row 41: Rep Row 17.

Row 42: Rep Row 14.

Row 43: Rep Row 15.

Rows 44–57: Using MC, ch 1, 92 sc, turn.

Fasten off MC after Row 57.

Rows 58–99: Rep Rows 14–57.

Fasten off.

BOTH PILLOWS

Finishing

Pull all yarn tails to the back side of the pillow and knot if desired.

Block to dimensions if desired.

With the RS of the pillow front and back facing out, work single crochet through both layers evenly around three edges of pillow, working three single crochet into each corner. Insert the pillow form and work single crochet evenly along the last side to close the opening. Weave in all ends.

LA PLATA
Rug & Pillow

The La Plata Mountains in southwest Colorado have 18 peaks above 12,000ft (3,657m), creating a breathtaking view on the drive from my house to the closest city of Durango, Colorado. La Plata means "the silver" in Spanish. Locals use the peaks as a landmark for navigation because they are visible from almost everywhere in the Four Corners area. The tallest peak is Hesperus Mountain or *Dibé Ntsaa* in Navajo. It is one of six mountains sacred to the Diné people and marks the northern boundary of the traditional Diné homeland.

The distinctive silhouette of the La Plata Mountains' snow-covered summits inspired the design of this textured rug and pillow. Bobble stitches give an irresistible squishiness that is a joy to touch and stand on. Use the rug in the kitchen, bedroom, bathroom, or entryway. The pillow is a quick project that packs a major texture payoff with bobble stiches in a classic diamond shape. Use bulky weight yarn to make an 18in (46cm) pillow or DK or worsted weight yarn for a more delicate 16in (41cm) pillow.

SUPPLIES

YARN

Rug: bulky (chunky) weight, 2,840yd (2,597m) plus 85yd (78m) for fringe

Worsted (aran) weight pillow: 760yd (695m)

Bulky (chunky) weight pillow: 810yd (741m) plus 17yd (15.5m) for fringe (optional)

Rug shown in Hoooked Wavy Blends (80% recycled cotton, 20% other recycled fibers); 284yd (260m)/250g: WB06 Caramel Taupe (10 balls)

Worsted yarn pillow shown in Dibe' be' iina (Sheep is Life) Navajo Nation yarn (100% Navajo Churro wool); 190yd (174m)/113g: White Heather (4 skeins)

Bulky yarn pillow shown in Hoooked Wavy Blends (80% recycled cotton, 20% other recycled fibers); 284yd (260m)/250g: WB06 Caramel Taupe (3 balls)

YARN ALTERNATIVES

Red Heart Super Saver, Patons Classic Wool Worsted, Brown Sheep Lamb's Pride Worsted, Cascade 220, Knit Picks Wool of the Andes Worsted, Stylecraft Special Aran, Lily Sugar 'n Cream cotton

HOOK

4mm (G/6) crochet hook for rug, 3.25mm (D/3) hook for pillow with worsted yarn, 4mm (G/6) hook for pillow with bulky yarn

GAUGE

Rug: 15 sts and 16 rows = 4in (10cm) in pattern

Worsted weight pillow: 18 sts and 18 rows = 4in (10cm) in pattern

Bulky weight pillow: 15 sts and 16 rows = 4in (10cm) in pattern

SIZE

Rug: 38 x 59in (97 x 150cm) not including fringe

Worsted weight pillow: 15in (38cm) square to fit a 16in (40.5cm) square pillow form

Bulky weight pillow: 17in (43cm) square to fit an 18in (46cm) square pillow form

Pattern Notes

The work is turned after each row. The turning chain does not count as a stitch. Each bobble is worked over two stitches: the bobble in the first stitch and a single crochet into the second stitch to close the bobble and make it pop toward the back of the work.

Bobble stitch: yarn over, insert hook into stitch, yarn over and pull through stitch, yarn over and pull through two loops (two loops on the hook), yarn over and insert hook into stitch, yarn over and pull through stitch, yarn over and pull through two loops (three loops on the hook), yarn over and insert hook into stitch, yarn over and pull through stitch, yarn over and pull through two loops (four loops on the hook), yarn over and insert hook into stitch, yarn over and pull through stitch, yarn over and pull through two loops (five loops on the hook), yarn over and pull through all five loops on hook, single crochet into next stitch.

RUG

Ch 145.

Row 1: Sc in 2nd ch from hook and each ch across, turn. (144 sts)

Row 2 and all even rows: Ch 1 (does not count as st), 144 sc.

Row 3: Ch 1, 6 sc, [3 bobbles, 10 sc] twice, 2 bobbles, 10 sc, 3 bobbles, 10 sc, 4 bobbles, 10 sc, 3 bobbles, 10 sc, 2 bobbles, [10 hdc, 3 bobbles] twice, 6 sc.

Row 5: Ch 1, [10 hdc, 3 bobbles] twice, 16 sc, 3 bobbles, 10 sc, 3 bobbles, 4 sc, 3 bobbles, 10 sc, 3 bobbles, 16 sc, [3 bobbles, 10 sc] twice.

Row 7: Ch 1, 2 sc, 1 bobble, [10 sc, 3 bobbles] twice, 8 sc, 3 bobbles, 10 sc, 3 bobbles, 12 sc, 3 bobbles, 10 sc, 3 bobbles, 8 sc, [3 bobbles, 10 sc] twice, 1 bobble, 2 sc.

Row 9: Ch 1, 2 sc, [3 bobbles, 10 sc] twice, 6 bobbles, 10 sc, 3 bobbles, 20 sc, 3 bobbles, 10 sc, 6 bobbles, [10 sc, 3 bobbles] twice, 2 sc.

Row 11: Rep Row 3

Row 13: Ch 1, [10 sc, 3 bobbles] twice, 16 sc, 3 bobbles, 10 sc, 3 bobbles, 4 sc, 3 bobbles, 10 sc, 3 bobbles, 16 sc, [3 bobbles, 10 sc] twice.

Row 15: Ch 1, 2 sc, 2 bobbles, [8 sc, 3 bobbles, 10 sc, 3 bobbles] twice, 12 sc, [3 bobbles, 10 sc, 3 bobbles, 8 sc] twice, 2 bobbles, 2 sc.

Row 17: Ch 1, 4 sc, 3 bobbles, 8 sc, 3 bobbles, 10 sc, 6 bobbles, 10 sc, 3 bobbles, 8 sc, 2 bobbles, 8 sc, 3 bobbles, 10 sc, 6 bobbles, 10 sc, 3 bobbles, 8 sc, 3 bobbles, 4 sc.

Row 19: Ch 1, [8 sc, 3 bobbles] twice, 10 sc, 2 bobbles, 10 sc, 3 bobbles, 8 sc, 6 bobbles, 8 sc, 3 bobbles, 10 sc, 2 bobbles, 10 sc, [3 bobbles, 8 sc] twice.

Row 21: Ch 1, 12 sc, 3 bobbles, 8 sc, 3 bobbles, 16 sc, [3 bobbles, 8 sc] 3 times, 3 bobbles, 16 sc, 3 bobbles, 8 sc, 3 bobbles, 12 sc.

Row 23: Ch 1, 2 sc, 2 bobbles, 10 sc, 3 bobbles, [8 sc, 3 bobbles] 3 times, 16 sc, [3 bobbles, 8 sc] 3 times, 3 bobbles, 10 sc, 2 bobbles, 2 sc.

Row 25: Ch 1, 4 sc, 3 bobbles, 10 sc, 3 bobbles, 8 sc, 6 bobbles, 8 sc, 3 bobbles, 10 sc, 2 bobbles, 10 sc, 3 bobbles, 8 sc, 6 bobbles, 8 sc, 3 bobbles, 10 sc, 3 bobbles, 4 sc.

Row 27: Ch 1, 8 sc, 3 bobbles, 10 sc, 3 bobbles, 8 sc, 2 bobbles, 8 sc, 3 bobbles, 10 sc, 6 bobbles, 10 sc, 3 bobbles, 8 sc, 2 bobbles, 8 sc, 3 bobbles, 10 sc, 3 bobbles, 8 sc.

Row 29: Ch 1, [12 sc, 3 bobbles, 10 sc, 3 bobbles] twice, 8 sc, [3 bobbles, 10 sc, 3 bobbles, 12 sc] twice.

Row 31: Ch 1, 2 sc, 2 bobbles, [10 sc, 3 bobbles] twice, 4 sc, 3 bobbles, 10 sc, 3 bobbles, 16 sc, 3 bobbles, 10 sc, 3 bobbles, 4 sc, [3 bobbles, 10 sc] twice, 2 bobbles, 2 sc.

Row 33: Ch 1, 4 sc, [3 bobbles, 10 sc] twice, 4 bobbles, 10 sc, 3 bobbles, 10 sc, 2 bobbles, 10 sc, 3 bobbles, 10 sc, 4 bobbles, [10 sc, 3 bobbles] twice, 4 sc.

Row 35: Rep Row 31.

Row 37: Rep Row 29.

Row 39: Rep Row 27.

Row 41: Rep Row 25.

Row 43: Rep Row 23.

Row 45: Rep Row 21.

Row 47: Rep Row 19.

Row 49: Rep Row 17.

Row 51: Rep Row 15.

Row 53: Rep Row 13.

Row 55: Rep Row 11.

Row 57: Rep Row 9.

Row 59: Rep Row 7.

Row 61: Rep Row 5.

Rows 63–122: Rep Rows 3–62.

Rows 123–184: Rep Rows 3–62.

Rows 185 and 186: Rep Row 2.

Fasten off.

PILLOW FRONT/BACK

(make 2)

Ch 65.

Row 1: Sc in 2nd ch from hook and each ch across, turn. (64 sts)

Row 2 and all even rows: Ch 1 (does not count as st), 64 sc.

Row 3: Ch 1, 1 bobble, 10 sc, 3 bobbles, 10 sc, 4 bobbles, 10 sc, 3 bobbles, 10 sc, 1 bobble.

Row 5: Ch 1, 8 sc, 3 bobbles, 10 sc, 3 bobbles, 4 sc, 3 bobbles, 10 sc, 3 bobbles, 8 sc.

Row 7: Ch 1, 4 sc, 3 bobbles, 10 sc, 3 bobbles, 12 sc, 3 bobbles, 10 sc, 3 bobbles, 4 sc.

Row 9: Ch 1, 3 bobbles, 10 sc, 3 bobbles, 20 sc, 3 bobbles, 10 sc, 3 bobbles.

Row 11: Rep Row 3.

Row 13: Rep Row 5.

Row 15: Rep Row 7.

Row 17: Ch 1, 3 bobbles, 10 sc, 3 bobbles, 8 sc, 2 bobbles, 8 sc, 3 bobbles, 10 sc, 3 bobbles.

Row 19: Ch 1, 1 bobble, 10 sc, 3 bobbles, 8 sc, 6 bobbles, 8 sc, 3 bobbles, 10 sc, 1 bobble.

Row 21: Ch 1, 8 sc, [3 bobbles, 8 sc] 4 times.

Row 23: Ch 1, 4 sc, 3 bobbles, 8 sc, 3 bobbles, 16 sc, 3 bobbles, 8 sc, 3 bobbles, 4 sc.

Row 25: Ch 1, 3 bobbles, 8 sc, 3 bobbles, 10 sc, 2 bobbles, 10 sc, 3 bobbles, 8 sc, 3 bobbles.

Row 27: Ch 1, 1 bobble, 8 sc, 3 bobbles, 10 sc, 6 bobbles, 10 sc, 3 bobbles, 8 sc, 1 bobble.

Row 29: Ch 1, 6 sc, 3 bobbles, 10 sc, 3 bobbles, 8 sc, 3 bobbles, 10 sc, 3 bobbles, 6 sc.

Row 31: Ch 1, 2 sc, 3 bobbles, 10 sc, 3 bobbles, 16 sc, 3 bobbles, 10 sc, 3 bobbles, 2 sc.

Row 33: Ch 1, 2 bobbles, 10 sc, 3 bobbles, 10 sc, 2 bobbles, 10 sc, 3 bobbles, 10 sc, 2 bobbles.

Row 35: Rep Row 31.

Row 37: Rep Row 29.

Row 39: Rep Row 27.

Row 41: Rep Row 25.

Row 43: Rep Row 23.

Row 45: Rep Row 21.

Row 47: Rep Row 19.

Row 49: Rep Row 17.

Row 51: Rep Row 15.

Row 53: Rep Row 13.

Row 55: Rep Row 11.

Row 57: Rep Row 9.

Row 59: Rep Row 7.

Row 61: Rep Row 5.

Row 63: Rep Row 3.

Row 64: Rep Row 2.

Border (Optional)

Round 1: Ch 1, sc evenly around working 3 sc into each corner st, sl st to first sc.

Fasten off.

Finishing

Pull any yarn tails to the back of the work and knot them. With the RS of the pillow front and back facing outward, attach the yarn at a corner with a slip stitch. Single crochet evenly around three sides, working through both front and back pieces and working three single crochet in each corner stitch. Insert the pillow form and continue to single crochet across. Slip stitch to the first stitch. Fasten off and weave in ends.

RUG AND PILLOW

Fringe (Optional)

For the rug, cut 292 pieces of yarn 10in (25.5cm) long. For the pillow, cut 232 pieces. To make fringe quickly, cut a piece of cardboard to about 5in (13cm) wide. A 5in (13cm)-wide gauge ruler makes a convenient tool to wrap fringe around. Wrap the yarn around; each wrap around creates one piece of fringe. Cut along one end only. Each cluster of fringes will contain four pieces of yarn. Starting at a corner of the short end of the rug or at the corner of the pillow, *insert the hook into the stitch from the back of the rug to the front, fold four pieces of yarn in half, grab the center with the hook, pull through about 2in (5cm), tuck the ends of the yarn through the loop, tighten the knot, skip the next stitch. Rep from * across. Trim one cluster of fringes at a time with sharp scissors.

Chart

Each square of the chart represents two stitches in one row.

Read all odd numbered (RS) rows from right to left. All even-numbered (WS) rows are single crochet.

Each white square represents two single crochet stitches, each X represents a bobble stitch.

Bobbles are worked over two stitches: the bobble in the first stitch and a single crochet in the second stitch.

KEY

- ☒ Bobble stitch
- ☐ 2 single crochet stitches
- ▭ Pillow chart

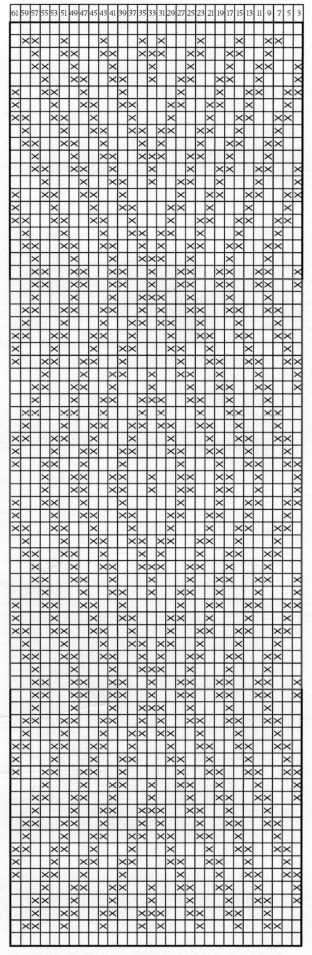

TOP OF CHART

DREAMER'S PATH
Wrap

There's a dreamy quality to the landscapes of the American southwest. Eagles and hawks sail across bright blue skies, prickly tumbleweeds roll across red dirt roads and fields of fragrant sage, delicate rock arches soar, formidable mountains inspire awe, and deeply forested valleys bring a sense of peace. The forces of nature sweep over it all and set these poetic landscapes in motion. Out here, you are free to gaze at the brilliance of the Milky Way and to choose your own dreamer's path.

This is a beautifully bohemian wrap for cool nights inspired by the otherworldly rock formations of the Bisti De-Na-Zin wilderness in northeast New Mexico, known locally as the Bisti badlands. The overlay mosaic crochet style turns the yarn ends into twisted fringe—no ends to weave in! Let the wandering path of this wrap's stitches inspire your next creative adventure.

SUPPLIES

YARN

DK weight in 2 colors

Main Color (MC): 1,023yd (935m)

Contrast Color (CC): 651yd (595m)

Shown in Rowan Handknit Cotton yarn (100% cotton); 93yd (85m)/50g: Ice Water (MC, 11 balls) and Atlantic (CC, 7 balls)

HOOK

4.5mm (US 7) crochet hook

GAUGE

14 sts and 16 rows = 4in (10cm) in pattern

SIZE

18½ x 77in (47 x 196cm)

Pattern Notes

This pattern is worked in overlay mosaic crochet. Each row is worked in one color of yarn: odd rows use MC; even rows use CC. The work is not turned; the right side is kept facing you throughout. The yarn is cut and fastened off after each row, leaving a 12in (30.5cm) tail at the start and end of each row to allow for the fringe. The new yarn is joined to the first stitch of the previous row with a slip stitch. Turning chains do not count as a stitch. All single crochet are worked into the back loop only except for the first and last stitches of each row. All double crochet are worked into the front loop only of the stitch two rows below.

WRAP

Using MC, ch 262.

Row 1: Dc in 3rd ch from hook and all ch across, fasten off. (260 sts)

Row 2 and all even rows: Using CC, ch 1 (does not count as a st), sc, 258 sc in BLO, sc, fasten off.

Rows 3, 5, and 7: Ch 1, sc, 258 dc, sc, fasten off.

Rows 9 and 11: Ch 1, sc, 8 dc, [2 sc, dc] 81 times, 7 dc, sc, fasten off.

Row 13: Ch 1, sc, 11 dc, *[2 sc, dc] 7 times, 3 dc; rep from * 9 more times, 7 dc, sc, fasten off.

Row 15: Ch 1, sc, 11 dc, *3 dc, [2 sc, dc] 5 times, 3 dc, 2 sc, 4 dc, [2 sc, dc] 5 times, 6 dc; rep from * 4 more times, 7 dc, sc, fasten off.

Row 17: Ch 1, sc, 11 dc, *6 dc, [2 sc, dc] 5 times, 3 dc, [2 sc, dc] 5 times, 9 dc; rep from * 4 more times, 7 dc, sc, fasten off.

Row 19: Ch 1, sc, 11 dc, *9 dc, [2 sc, dc] 9 times, 12 dc; rep from * 4 more times, 7 dc, sc, fasten off.

Row 21: Ch 1, sc, 11 dc, *12 dc, [2 sc, dc] 7 times, 15 dc; rep from * 4 more times, 7 dc, sc, fasten off.

Reminder

• Use MC for odd rows and CC for even rows.

• All single crochet are worked into the BLO except the first and last stitches of each row.

• All double crochet stitches are worked into the FLO two rows below.

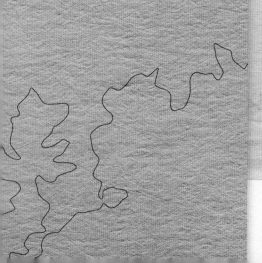

Row 23: Ch 1, sc, 8 dc, 2 sc, *16 dc, [2 sc, dc] 5 times, 15 dc, 2 sc; rep from * 4 more times, 8 dc, sc, fasten off.

Row 25: Ch 1, sc, 8 dc, *[2 sc, dc] twice, 15 dc, 2 sc, dc; rep from * 9 more times, 2 sc, 8 dc, sc, fasten off.

Row 27: Ch 1, sc, 8 dc, 2 sc, dc, *(2 sc, dc) twice, 15 dc, 2 sc, 16 dc, [2 sc, dc] 3 times; rep from * 4 more times, 7 dc, sc, fasten off.

Row 29: Ch 1, sc, 8 dc, 2 sc, dc, *[2 sc, dc] 3 times, 27 dc, [2 sc, dc] 4 times; rep from * 4 more times, 7 dc, sc, fasten off.

Row 31: Ch 1, sc, 8 dc, 2 sc, dc, *[2 sc, dc] 4 times, 21 dc, [2 sc, dc] 5 times; rep from * 4 more times, 7 dc, sc, fasten off.

Row 33: Ch 1, sc, 11 dc, *[2 sc, dc] 5 times, 15 dc, [2 sc, dc] 5 times, 3 dc, rep from * 4 more times; 7 dc, sc, fasten off.

Row 35: Ch 1, sc, 11 dc, *3 dc, [2 sc, dc] 5 times, 9 dc, [2 sc, dc] 5 times, 6 dc, rep from * 4 more times; 7 dc, sc, fasten off.

Row 37: Ch 1, sc, 11 dc, *6 dc, [2 sc, dc] 5 times, 3 dc, [2 sc, dc] 5 times, 9 dc, rep from * 4 more times; 7 dc, sc, fasten off.

Row 39: Ch 1, sc, 11 dc, *9dc, [2 sc, dc] 9 times, 12 dc; rep from * 4 more times, 7 dc, sc, fasten off.

Row 41: Rep Row 37.

Row 43: Rep Row 35.

Row 45: Rep Row 33.

Row 47: Rep Row 31.

Row 49: Rep Row 29.

Row 51: Rep Row 27.

Row 53: Rep Row 25.

Row 55: Rep Row 23.

Row 57: Rep Row 21.

Row 59: Rep Row 19.

Row 61: Rep Row 17.

Row 63: Rep Row 15.

Row 65: Rep Row 13.

Rows 67 and 69: Rep Row 9.

Rows 71, 73, 75, and 77: Rep Row 3.

Fasten off.

Finishing

Block to dimensions if desired. Trim yarn tails at the start and end of each row to 11in (28cm).

For a twisted fringe, gather the ends from Rows 1 and 3 in one hand and the ends from Rows 5 and 7 in the other hand. Twist both groups of yarn in the same direction, either clockwise or counterclockwise, until the yarn begins to kink. Tie the two groups of two twisted tails together in an overhand knot about 6in (15cm) from the edge of the wrap to create one twisted fringe containing four yarn tails. Trim the yarn ends ½in (1cm) below the knot. Repeat with the ends from Rows 2 and 4 in one hand and the ends from Rows 6 and 8 in the other. Repeat with the rest of the yarn tails.

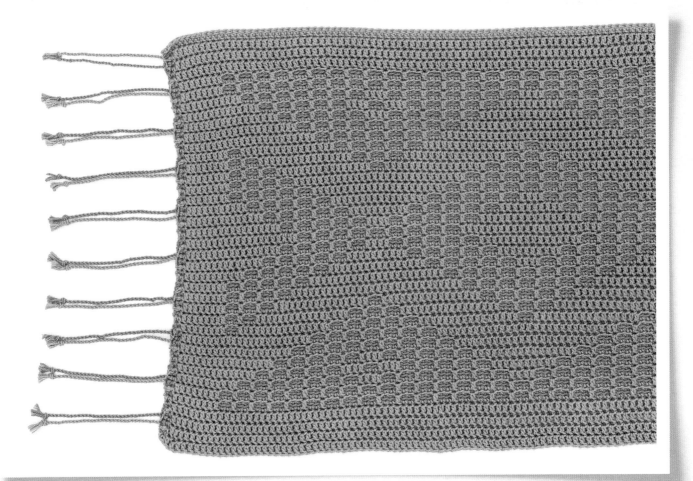

VALLEY OF DREAMS
Blanket

This pattern is inspired by a unique rock formation known as the Alien Throne in the remote Valley of Dreams in the Ah-Shi-Sle-Pah Wilderness in northwest New Mexico. The name Ah-Shi-Sle-Pah comes from the Navajo words *áshįh ibá* meaning "gray salt". This otherworldly wilderness is far from any cities, paved roads, phone signal, or even marked trails. The towering rock formations offer an inspiring place to relax and dream.

Alien Throne, Valley of Dreams, New Mexico

This one-of-a-kind blanket combines filet crochet lace with bobble stitches for irresistible texture and unforgettable style.

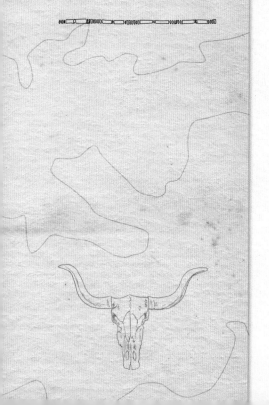

SUPPLIES

YARN

Worsted (aran) weight, 1,500yd (1,372m)

Shown in Dibe' be' iina (Sheep is Life) Navajo Nation yarn (100% Navajo Churro wool); 190yd (174m)/113g: White Heather (8 skeins)

YARN ALTERNATIVES

Patons Classic Wool Worsted, Brown Sheep Lamb's Pride Worsted, Cascade 220, Knit Picks Wool of the Andes Worsted, Stylecraft Special Aran, Lily Sugar 'n Cream cotton

HOOK

5.5mm (I/9) crochet hook

GAUGE

3 sts and 7 rows = 4in (10cm) in dc

SIZE

36 x 48in (91 x 122cm)

Pattern Notes

Bobble stitches are worked over two stitches: the bobble in the first stitch and a single crochet in the second stitch to close the bobble and make it pop toward the back of the work. When crocheting along the open spaces created by the ch-2 from the previous row, single crochet into the ch-2 space twice instead of crocheting into the tiny chain stitches. This helps open up the filet crochet lace.

Bobble stitch: yarn over, insert hook into stitch, yarn over and pull through stitch, yarn over and pull through two loops (two loops on the hook), yarn over and insert hook into stitch, yarn over and pull through stitch, yarn over and pull through two loops (three loops on the hook), yarn over and insert hook into stitch, yarn over and pull through stitch, yarn over and pull through two loops (four loops on the hook), yarn over and insert hook into stitch, yarn over and pull through stitch, yarn over and pull through two loops (five loops on the hook), yarn over and pull through all five loops on hook, single crochet into next stitch.

BLANKET

Ch 110.

Row 1: Dc in 3rd ch from hook and each ch across, turn. (108 sts)

Rows 2–6: Ch 3 (counts as first st here and throughout), 107 dc.

Row 7: Ch 3, dc in next 5 sts, [ch 2, skip 2 sts, dc in next st] twice (2 open spaces made), bobble st, dc in next 12 sts, bobble st, dc in next st, [ch 2, skip 2 sts, dc in next st] 5 times (5 open spaces made), bobble st, dc in next 16 sts, bobble st, dc in next st, [ch 2, skip 2 sts, dc in next st] 5 times (5 open spaces made), bobble st, dc in next 12 sts, bobble st, dc in next st, [ch 2, skip 2, dc in next st] twice (2 open spaces made), dc in last 5 sts.

Row 8 and all even rows through Row 104: Ch 1 (does not count as st), sc in same st and each st across, working 2 sc into each ch–2 space.

Row 9: Ch 3, dc in next 5 sts, [ch 2, skip 2 sts, dc in next st] 3 times (3 open spaces made), bobble st, dc in next 12 sts, bobble st, dc in next st, [ch 2, skip 2 sts, dc in next st] 5 times (5 open spaces made), bobble st, dc in next 10 sts, bobble st, dc in next st, [ch 2, skip 2 sts, dc in next st] 5 times (5 open spaces made), bobble st, dc in next 12 sts, bobble st, dc in next st, [ch 2, skip 2 sts, dc in next st] 3 times (3 open spaces made), dc in last 5 sts.

Row 11: Ch 3, dc in next 5 sts, [ch 2, skip 2 sts, dc in next st] 4 times (4 open spaces made), bobble st, dc in next 12 sts, bobble st, dc in next st, [ch 2, skip 2 sts, dc in next st] 5 times (5 open spaces made), bobble st, dc in next 4 sts, bobble st, dc in next st, [ch 2, skip 2 sts, dc in next st] 5 times (5 open spaces made), bobble st, dc in next 12 sts, bobble st, dc in next st, [ch 2, skip 2 sts, dc in next st] 4 times (4 open spaces made), dc in last 5 sts.

Row 13: Ch 3, dc in next 5 sts, [ch 2, skip 2 sts, dc in next st] 5 times (5 open spaces made), bobble st, dc in next 12 sts, bobble st, dc in next st, [ch 2, skip 2 sts, dc in next st] 5 times (5 open spaces made), bobble st, dc in next st, [ch 2, skip 2 sts, dc in next st] 5 times (5 open spaces made), bobble st, dc in next 12 sts, bobble st, dc in next st, [ch 2, skip 2 sts, dc in next st] 5 times (5 open spaces made), dc in last 5 sts.

Row 15: Ch 3, dc in next 5 sts, [ch 2, skip 2 sts, dc in next st] 6 times (6 open spaces made), bobble st, dc in next 12 sts, bobble st, dc in next st, [ch 2, skip 2 sts, dc in next st] 9 times (9 open spaces made), bobble st, dc in next 12 sts, bobble st, dc in next st, [ch 2, skip 2 sts, dc in next st] 6 times (6 open spaces made), dc in last 5 sts.

Row 17: Ch 3, dc in next 5 sts, [ch 2, skip 2 sts, dc in next st] 7 times (7 open spaces made), bobble st, dc in next 12 sts, bobble st, dc in next st, [ch 2, skip 2 sts, dc in next st] 7 times (7 open spaces made), bobble st, dc in next 12 sts, bobble st, dc in next st, [ch 2, skip 2 sts, dc in next st] 7 times (7 open spaces made), dc in last 5 sts.

Row 19: Ch 3, dc in next 5 sts, [ch 2, skip 2 sts, dc in next st] 8 times (8 open spaces made), bobble st, dc in next 12 sts, bobble st, dc in next st, [ch 2, skip 2 sts, dc in next st] 5 times (5 open spaces made), bobble st, dc in next 12 sts, bobble st, dc in next st, [ch 2, skip 2 sts, dc in next st] 8 times (8 open spaces made), dc in last 5 sts.

In Row 21, we start to add the little bobble flower motif in the open mesh sections at the right and left sides of the work.

Row 21: Ch 3, dc in next 5 sts, [ch 2, skip 2 sts, dc in next st] 3 times (3 open spaces made), bobble st, dc in next st, [ch 2, skip 2 sts, dc in next st] 5 times (5 open spaces made), bobble st, dc in next 12 sts, bobble st, dc in next st, [ch 2, skip 2 sts, dc in next st] 3 times (3 open spaces made) bobble st, dc in next 12 sts, bobble st, dc in next st, [ch 2, skip 2 sts, dc in next st] 5 times (5 open spaces made), bobble st, dc in next st, [ch 2, skip 2 sts, dc in next st] 3 times (3 open spaces made), dc in last 5 sts.

Row 23: Ch 3, dc in next 5 sts, [ch 2, skip 2 sts, dc in next st] twice (2 open spaces made), bobble st, dc in next st, [ch 2, skip 2 sts, dc in next st] once (1 open space made), bobble st, dc in next st, [ch 2, skip 2 sts, dc in next st] 5 times (5 open spaces made), bobble st, dc in next 12 sts, bobble st, dc in next st, [ch 2, skip 2 sts, dc in next st] once (1 open space made), bobble st, dc in next 12 sts, bobble st, dc in next st, [ch 2, skip 2 sts, dc in next st] 5 times (5 open spaces made), bobble st, dc in next st, [ch 2, skip 2 sts, dc in next st] once (1 open space made),

bobble st, dc in next st, [ch 2, skip 2 sts, dc in next st] twice (2 open spaces made), dc in last 5 sts.

In Row 25, the path of 12 dc on each side starts to zigzag back out toward the edges.

Row 25: Rep Row 21.

Row 27: Rep Row 19.

Row 29: Rep Row 17.

Row 31: Rep Row 15.

Row 33: Rep Row 13.

Row 35: Rep Row 11.

Row 37: Rep Row 9.

Rows 39–70: Rep Rows 7–38.

Rows 71–102: Rep Rows 7–38.

Row 103: Rep Row 7.

Rows 105–110: Rep Row 2.

Fasten off.

Finishing

Weave in all ends.

Block if desired.

CACTUS GARDEN
Blanket

Some of the most iconic plant species of the American southwest are cacti. The Four Corners area is home to dozens of cactus species including prickly pear, cholla, claret cup, fishhook, and pin-cushion cactus. The Durango Botanic Gardens along the Animas River hosts a gorgeous rock garden that features many native species. Mesa Verde National Park near Mancos, Colorado is a lovely place to take a plant walk and enjoy dozens of cactus species, beautiful white sage bushes, yucca, juniper, and other high desert plants.

This pattern is an invitation to collaborate with a friend. I began stitching this blanket, then passed it to my twin sister Karen, who stitched a few repeats. Then she passed it back to me to finish the blanket. Share a similar blanket-making experience with a friend or loved one who crochets. The stitches may not be perfectly uniform because each crocheter has their own unique style and rhythm (even identical twins!). Luckily, perfection isn't the goal—it's about sharing the experience of making something together and being reminded of the other person when you look at the finished project.

SUPPLIES

YARN
DK weight in two colors

Main Color (MC): 1,985yd (1,815m)

Contrast Color (CC): 1,635yd (1,495m)

Shown in Hoooked Somen (60% recycled cotton yarn, 40% linen); 180yd (165m)/100g: Avocado (MC, 11 skeins) and Oliva (CC, 10 skeins)

HOOK
5mm (H/8) crochet hook for blanket, 4mm (G/6) hook for border

GAUGE
16 sts and 16 rows = 4in (10cm)

SIZE
43 x 60in (109 x 152cm)

Pattern Notes

The pattern is worked in overlay mosaic crochet. Each row is worked in one color of yarn. Odd rows use MC, include both single and double crochet stitches, and form the diamond pattern. Even rows use CC. The work is not turned; always work from right to left and keep the right side of the blanket facing up. Left-handed crocheters will always work from left to right. The yarn is cut and fastened off after each row, leaving a 4in (10cm) tail at the start and end of each row. The new yarn is joined to the first stitch of the previous row with a slip stitch. A simple two-round border covers the yarn ends and creates a cord-like edging. If you would rather make fringe, leave a 8-10in (20-25.5cm) tail at the start and end of each row. If you are not sure whether you want fringe or a border, leave long tails just in case. All single crochet are in the BLO except the first and last stitches of each row, which are through both loops; all double crochet are in the FLO of the row below.

BLANKET

Using MC, ch 197.

Row 1: Sc into 2nd ch from hook and each ch across, fasten off, do not turn. (196 sts)

Row 2 and all even rows: Using CC, ch 1 (does not count as a st here or throughout), sc, 194 sc in BLO, sc, fasten off, do not turn.

Row 3: Ch 1, sc, sc in BLO, [4 dc, 10 sc, 6 dc, 10 sc, 4 dc, 10 sc, 6 dc, 10 sc, 4 dc] 3 times, sc in BLO, sc.

Row 5: Ch 1, sc, sc in BLO, [2 sc, 6 dc, 10 sc, 6 dc, 16 sc, 6 dc, 10 sc, 6 dc, 2 sc] 3 times, sc in BLO, sc.

Row 7: Ch 1, sc, sc in BLO, [6 sc, 6 dc, 10 sc, 6 dc, 8 sc, 6 dc, 10 sc, 6 dc, 6 sc] 3 times, sc in BLO, sc.

Row 9: Ch 1, sc, sc in BLO, [10 sc, 6 dc, 10 sc, 12 dc, 10 sc, 6 dc, 10 sc] 3 times, sc in BLO, sc.

Row 11: Ch 1, sc, sc in BLO, [4 dc, 10 sc, 6 dc, 10 sc, 4 dc, 10 sc, 6 dc, 10 sc, 4 dc] 3 times, sc in BLO, sc.

Row 13: Ch 1, sc, sc in BLO, [2 sc, 6 dc, 10 sc, 6 dc, 16 sc, 6 dc, 10 sc, 6 dc, 2 sc] 3 times, sc in BLO, sc.

Row 15: Ch 1, sc, sc in BLO, [6 sc, 6 dc, 10 sc, 6 dc, 8 sc, 6 dc, 10 sc, 6 dc, 6 sc] 3 times, sc in BLO, sc.

Reminder

• Use MC for odd rows and CC for even rows.

• All single crochet are worked into the BLO except the first and last stitches of each row

• All double crochet stitches are worked into the FLO two rows below.

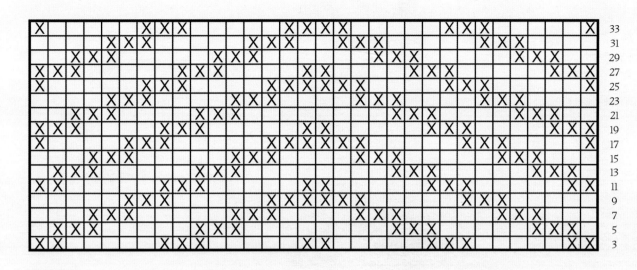

KEY

☒ 2 dc in FLO 2 rows below

☐ 2 sc in BLO

Row 17: Ch 1, sc, sc in BLO, [2 dc, 8 sc, 6 dc, 10 sc, 12 dc, 10 sc, 6 dc, 8 sc, 2 dc] 3 times, sc in BLO, sc.

Row 19: Ch 1, sc, sc in BLO, [6 dc, 8 sc, 6 dc, 10 sc, 4 dc, 10 sc, 6 dc, 8 sc, 6 dc] 3 times, sc in BLO, sc.

Row 21: Ch 1, sc, sc in BLO, [4 sc, 6 dc, 8 sc, 6 dc, 16 sc, 6 dc, 8 sc, 6 dc, 4 sc] 3 times, sc in BLO, sc.

Row 23: Ch 1, sc, sc in BLO, *[8 sc, 6 dc] 4 times, 8 sc; rep from * twice more, sc in BLO, sc.

Row 25: Ch 1, sc, sc in BLO, [2 dc, 10 sc, 6 dc, 8 sc, 12 dc, 8 sc, 6 dc, 10 sc, 2 dc] 3 times, sc in BLO, sc.

Row 27: Ch 1, sc, sc in BLO, [6 dc, 10 sc, 6 dc, 8 sc, 4 dc, 8 sc, 6 dc, 10 sc, 6 dc] 3 times, sc in BLO, sc.

Row 29: Ch 1, sc, sc in BLO, [4 sc, 6 dc, 10 sc, 6 dc, 12 sc, 6 dc, 10 sc, 6 dc, 4 sc] 3 times, sc in BLO, sc.

Row 31: Ch 1, sc, sc in BLO, [8 sc, 6 dc, 10 sc, 6 dc, 4 sc, 6 dc, 10 sc, 6 dc, 8 sc] 3 times, sc in BLO, sc.

Row 33: Ch 1, sc, sc in BLO, [2 dc, 10 sc, 6 dc, 10 sc, 8 dc, 10 sc, 6 dc, 10 sc, 2 dc] 3 times, sc in BLO, sc.

Rows 35 and 36: Rep Rows 31 and 32.

Rows 37 and 38: Rep Rows 29 and 30.

Rows 39 and 40: Rep Rows 27 and 28.

Rows 41 and 42: Rep Rows 25 and 26.

Rows 43 and 44: Rep Rows 23 and 24.

Rows 45 and 46: Rep Rows 21 and 22.

Rows 47 and 48: Rep Rows 19 and 20.

Rows 49 and 50: Rep Rows 17 and 18.

Rows 51 and 52: Rep Rows 15 and 16.

Rows 53 and 54: Rep Rows 13 and 14.

Rows 55 and 56: Rep Rows 11 and 12.

Rows 57 and 58: Rep Rows 9 and 10.

Rows 59 and 60: Rep Rows 7 and 8.

Rows 61 and 62: Rep Rows 5 and 6.

Rows 63–122: Rep Rows 3–62.

Rows 123–182: Rep Rows 3–62.

Rows 183–242: Rep Rows 3–62.

Row 243: Rep Row 3.

Fasten off.

Chart

Each square of the chart represents two stitches in the same row.

The chart is symmetrical so odd-numbered rows can be read from right to left or left to right. All even-numbered rows are single crochet through the back loop only.

Each X represents two double crochet stitches into the odd row below. Each blank square represents two single crochet stitches.

The first two single crochet stitches of each row and the last two single crochet stitches of each row are not shown in the chart.

The chart repeats three times in each row.

Border

This is a very simple border of two rounds to cover the yarn ends from each row. Round 1 is all single crochet, with one stitch into the end of each row and one stitch into each stitch on the short ends of the blanket. The yarn tails from the end of each row get hidden inside the single crochet stitches of Round 1. Round 2 is reverse single crochet (crab stitch) around the Round 1 stitches to double-wrap the yarn ends. The border uses a hook size 1mm smaller than the hook size for the rest of the blanket. If you used a 5mm (H/8) hook for the blanket, use a 4mm (G/6) hook for the border. You can tug a bit to straighten the edge, but do not pull too hard or your border may become wavy. If your border starts to get waves, try using a smaller crochet hook.

Border Preparation

Trim the yarn tails from each row to about 2in (5cm). This reduces the bulk of the yarn ends so you can crochet over and around them but leaves the ends long enough to be held securely under the two border rounds.

Round 1: Attach CC yarn with a sl st a few stitches from a corner on one short end of the blanket, sc in each st to corner, *work 3 sc into corner st, sc in end of each row along long edge of blanket, holding yarn ends tight together and close to blanket as you crochet over and around yarn ends to cover them as if they were carried yarn, 3 sc into corner, sc into each st along short end of blanket, rep from * around, sl st to first sc, do not fasten off (A, B).

Round 2: Reverse single crochet evenly around blanket, crocheting around Round 1 stitches on the long edges of the blanket to double-wrap the yarn ends. (C, D)

Fasten off and weave in ends. (E)

BABY BLANKET VARIATION

To make a baby blanket, you will need 590yd (540m) MC and 476yd (435m) CC yarn.

Chain 133 to create 132 sc in Row 1. Each row will have 132 stitches. Work only two pattern repeats per row instead of three. After Row 122, work Row 2, then Row 3, then proceed to the Border.

The finished dimensions of the blanket will be about 30in (76cm) square.

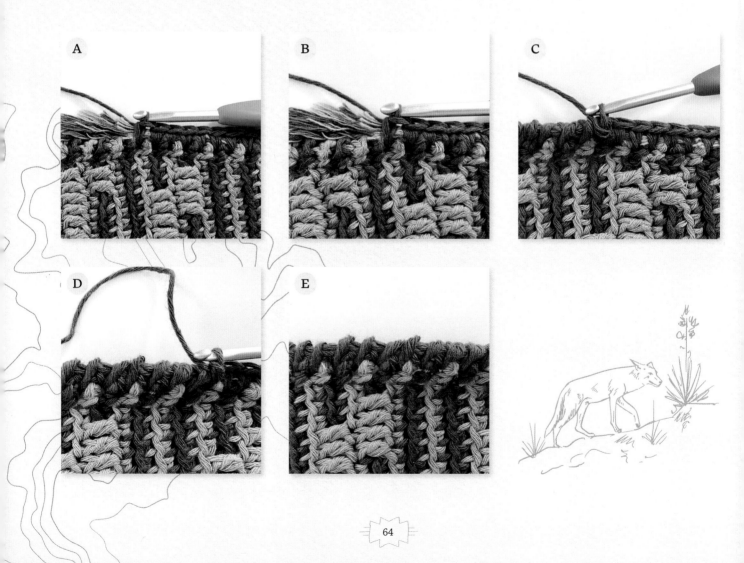

BEARS EARS
Fringed Pillow

The Bears Ears are a matching set of buttes in the canyonlands of southeast Utah. Surrounded by miles of protected wilderness, their appearance is so much like a bear's ears popping up over the horizon that they have the same name in all four languages of the local indigenous people. The Bears Ears area has thousands of sacred cultural and archeological sites dating as far back as 12,000 BCE. The Bears Ears National Monument was established in 2016 thanks to the Bears Ears Inter-Tribal Coalition of Hopi, Navajo, Ute Mountain Ute, Pueblo of Zuni, and Ute Indian tribe leaders.

This unique bohemian pillow is inspired by the playful spirit of the bear. Easy single crochet rows form the base of the pillow. Fringe is added to the ridged rows after joining the pillow front and back. The short fringe is a great way to use up small yarn scraps. It's an irresistibly touchable way to add textural interest to your living room or bedroom.

Bears roam throughout southwest Colorado each summer, feasting on acorns, berries, and fish before hibernating in autumn. The Ute and Diné people refrain from beating drums during winter while bears are sleeping. In traditional Diné teachings, the first thunder of spring is an invitation to go outside and stretch like the bears emerging from winter dens. The annual spring Bear Dance hosted by the Southern Ute tribe celebrates the bears' return and winter's end with ceremony, drumming, and dance. Participants are invited to leave behind winter's worries for a fresh start to spring.

SUPPLIES

YARN

Worsted (aran) weight in three colors

Main Color (MC): 450yd (411.5m) for pillow front and back plus 50yd (46m) for fringe

Contrast Color 1 (CC1): 33yd (30m)

Contrast Color 2 (CC2): 60yd (55m)

Shown in Dibe' be' iina (Sheep is Life) Navajo Nation yarn (100% Navajo Churro wool); 190yd (174m)/113g: White Heather (MC, 3 skeins), Light Gray (CC1, 1 skein), and Gray (CC2, 1 skein)

YARN ALTERNATIVES

Patons Classic Wool Worsted, Brown Sheep Lamb's Pride Worsted, Cascade 220, Knit Picks Wool of the Andes Worsted, Stylecraft Special Aran

OTHER MATERIALS

12 x 16in (30.5 x 41cm) pillow form

HOOK

4mm (G/6) crochet hook

GAUGE

17 sts and 19 rows = 4in (10cm) in sc

SIZE

11 x 15in (28 x 38cm) to fit a 12 x 16in (30.5 x 41cm) pillow form

Pattern Notes

The pillow front and back are identical before fringe is added to the front. Both pieces are a single crochet rectangle with alternating "ridge rows" and "plain rows". Ridge rows are created by crocheting into the back loop only of each stitch. Plain rows are worked into both loops of the stitch as usual. The fringe is attached to every ridge row to create 13 fringed rows. Use the chart as a guide for fringe placement or arrange the fringe however you like. Create two rows of each color, vertical stripes, symbols, freeform shapes... anything goes!

PILLOW FRONT/BACK

(make 2)

Ch 65.

Row 1: Sc in 2nd ch from hook and each ch, turn. (64 sts)

Row 2 (plain row): Ch 1 (does not count as st), 64 sc, turn.

Row 3: Rep Row 2.

Row 4 (ridge row): Ch 1, 64 sc in BLO, turn.

Rows 5–7: Rep Row 2.

Row 8: Rep Row 4.

Rows 9–52: Rep Rows 5–8.

Fasten off.

Finishing

With the ridged rows of the pillow front and back facing out, crochet evenly around three sides of both the front and back of the pillow, working 3 sc into each corner stitch. Fasten off.

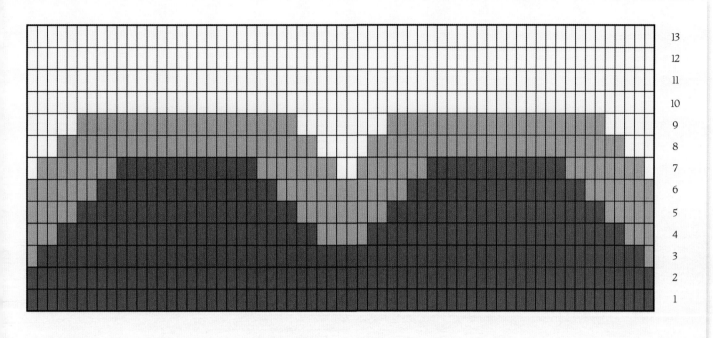

KEY

☐ MC   ▨ CC1   ▩ CC2

Chart

Each square represents one piece of fringe attached to the front loop of one single crochet stitch.

Fringe

Cut 832 pieces of yarn 5in (13cm) long: 292 pieces in MC, 190 pieces in CC1, and 350 pieces in CC2. Use the chart as a guide for color placement. Insert a hook into the front loop of the first stitch on the RS of the first ridge row at the bottom of the pillow front. Fold one piece of fringe in half and grab the center with the hook. Pull through the stitch (A) about 1in (2.5cm). Tuck the tails of the fringe down through the loop and pull to tighten (B). Repeat the process for the rest of the fringes (C).

Trim the fringes one row at a time. Insert the pillow form and single crochet through both the front and back of the pillow to close the opening.

Fasten off and weave in ends.

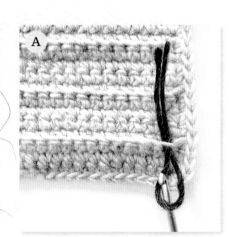

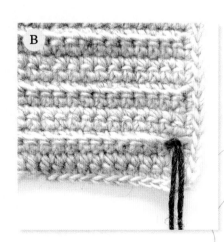

SOUTHWESTERN TAPESTRY

One of the hallmarks of southwestern textiles is the combination of colors and geometric patterns. You won't find any single-color rugs or blankets out here! My favorite style of southwestern tapestry crochet celebrates both natural colors and bold, bright colors in single or double crochet.

Two types of tapestry crochet are included here: projects with just two colors where both colors of yarn are carried throughout the whole piece, and projects with several colors where each section of color is created from its own small ball of yarn.

Beginners to crochet colorwork should try the two-color style first to practice switching back and forth between two yarns in the same row. The smaller Raider Ridge Wall Hanging is a great first tapestry crochet project because it's small and can be finished in a weekend. You can also turn it into a pillow by skipping the hanging loop row and omitting the fringe. The Land of Enchantment Blanket & Pillow and Lone Mesa Pillows & Tote are also easy projects for beginners. To showcase a gradient or ombré yarn, try the Canyon Moon Blanket or the Globe Trekker Throw in laid-back double crochet.

Beginners will feel the alluring call of working with more colors before too long! The challenge in tapestry crochet using many colors is managing the small balls of yarn so they do not tangle. The easiest way to avoid tangles is to pay attention when you turn your work after each row. Turn the left-hand side of your work over toward the right-hand side after one row, then turn the right-hand side of your work over toward the left-hand side after the next row. This allows you to keep the balls of yarn in a neat row in front of you while you crochet.

The Vallecito Blanket and the Wind River Weighted Blanket are the most technically challenging patterns of the book because of their use of many colors, but the payoff is impressive! These patterns can create heirloom-quality gifts to be treasured for generations.

RAIDER RIDGE
Wall Hangings

Raider Ridge forms the natural eastern boundary of the southwestern mountain town of Durango, Colorado. The Raider Ridge trail is a rough, rocky single track running directly up the steep spine of the ridge; if you brave it you are rewarded with gorgeous views of the Animas River. It's an amazing place to watch the sun set over the town, or to watch thrill-seeking mountain bikers launch themselves off ledges at full speed. It has been the proving ground for Durango mountain bike legends for generations.

Raider Ridge, Durango, Colorado

The adventurous spirit and rugged beauty of Durango inspired these luxurious wall hangings. The serrated diamond motif is a common one around the world; here in the southwest, you find it on textiles, ranch fences, buildings, clothing, and jewelry. It is sometimes called an Anatolian star or *yildiz* and can symbolize happiness. Made with super bulky yarn, it provides luxe soundproofing for a noisy hallway or soothing eye candy for a covered outdoor seating area. You can substitute three strands of worsted weight yarn held together for the super bulky yarn to make this project a scrap-friendly stash buster.

SUPPLIES

YARN

Super bulky (super chunky) weight in at least two colors

Small: Main Color 1 (MC1) 90yd (82m), Main Color 2 (MC2) 90yd (82m), Contrast Color (CC) 90yd (82m)

Large: Main Color 1 (MC1) 90yd (82m), Main Color 2 (MC2) 90yd (82m), Main Color 3 (MC3) 90yd (82m), Main Color 4 (MC4) 54yd (49m), Main Color 5 (MC5) 54yd (49m), Main Color 6 (MC6) 71yd (65m), Main Color 7 (MC7) 90yd (82m), Contrast Color (CC) 90yd (82m)

Shown in Malabrigo Rasta (100% merino wool); 90yd (82m)/150g:
Small: 150 Azul Profundo (MC1, 1 skein), 856 Azules (MC2, 1 skein), 063 Natural (CC, 1 skein)
Large: 868 Coronilla (MC1, 1 skein), 853 Abril (MC2, 1 skein), 611 Ravelry Red (MC3, 1 skein), 096 Sunset (MC4, 1 skein), 037 Lettuce (MC5, 1 skein), 809 Solis (MC6, 1 skein), 247 Whale's Road (MC7, 1 skein), 063 Natural (CC, 2 skeins)

YARN ALTERNATIVES

Bernat Blanket, Lion Brand Wool Ease Thick and Quick, Hoooked Zpagetti

OTHER MATERIALS

Small: 23in (58cm)-long, ¾in (2cm) diameter dowel

Large: 29½in (75cm)-long, ¾in (2cm) diameter dowel

HOOK

6.5mm (K/10½) crochet hook

GAUGE

10 sts and 10 rows = 4in (10cm) in sc

SIZE

Small: 13.5 x 18in (34 x 46cm) not including fringe

Large: 22 x 36in (56 x 91cm)

Pattern Notes

To change colors, yarn over with the new color to complete the last stitch in the old color.

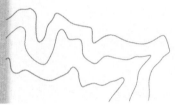

SMALL WALL HANGING

Using MC1, ch 43.

Row 1: Sc in 2nd ch from hook and all ch across, turn. (42 sts)

Row 2: Using MC1, ch 1 (does not count as st), 42 sc, turn.

Rows 3–32: Rep Row 2, following written Color Change Instructions or chart.

Row 33: Ch 1, sc, [ch 6, skip next st, sc in next 3 sts] 10 times, ch 6, sc. (11 hanging loops made)

Fasten off.

Color Change Instructions

Rows 1–4: 42 sc MC1.

Row 5: 42 sc MC2.

Row 6: 15 MC1, 12 CC, 15 MC1.

Row 7: 16 MC1, 10 CC, 16 MC1.

Row 8: 17 MC1, 8 CC, 17 MC1.

Row 9: 12 MC2, 6 CC, 6 MC2, 6 CC, 12 MC2.

Row 10: 13 MC2, 6 CC, 4 MC2, 6 CC, 13 MC2.

Row 11: 14 MC1, 6 CC, 2 MC1, 6 CC, 14 MC1.

Row 12: 8 MC1, 7 CC, 12 MC1, 7 CC, 8 MC1.

Row 13: 9 MC2, 7 CC, 10 MC2, 7 CC, 9 MC2.

Row 14: 10 MC2, 7 CC, 8 MC2, 7 CC, 10 MC2.

Row 15: 3 MC2, 8 CC, 20 MC2, 8 CC, 3 MC2.

Row 16: 4 MC1, 8 CC, 18 MC1, 8 CC, 4 MC1.

Row 17: 5 MC1, 8 CC, 16 MC1, 8 CC, 5 MC1.

Row 18: Rep Row 16.

Row 19: Rep Row 15.

Row 20: Rep Row 14.

Row 21: Rep Row 13.

Row 22: Rep Row 12.

Row 23: Rep Row 11.

Row 24: Rep Row 10.

Row 25: Rep Row 9.

Row 26: Rep Row 8.

Row 27: Rep Row 7.

Row 28: Rep Row 6.

Row 29: 42 sc MC2.

Rows 30–32: 42 sc MC1.

Row 33: 42 sc MC2.

.

Fringe for Small Wall Hanging (Optional)

Cut 63 pieces of yarn, each 24in (61cm) long in the color of your choice. Each cluster of fringes will contain three pieces of yarn. Starting at a corner of Row 1, insert the hook into the first stitch from the back of your work to the front. Fold three pieces of yarn in half and grab the center with the hook. Pull this loop through about 2in (5cm). Tuck the ends of the yarn through the loop and tighten the knot. Skip the next stitch. Rep across to create 21 clusters of fringes. Trim the fringe to about 10in (25.5cm) or as desired.

Small Wall Hanging Chart

Each square represents one single crochet stitch.

The chart is symmetrical and can be read from right to left or left to right.

KEY

☐ CC   ■ MC1   ■ MC2

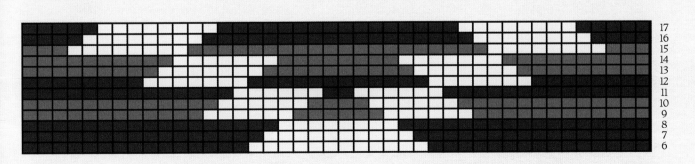

LARGE WALL HANGING

Using MC1, ch 60.

Row 1: Sc in 2nd ch from hook and all ch across, turn. (59 sts)

Row 2: Using MC1, ch 1 (does not count as st), 59 sc, turn. (59 sts)

Rows 3–90: Rep Row 2, following written Color Change Instructions or chart.

Row 91: Ch 1, sc, [ch 6, skip next st, sc in next 3 sts] 10 times, ch 6, sc. (15 hanging loops made)

Fasten off.

Color Change Instructions

Row 1: 59 sc MC1.

Row 2: 59 sc MC2.

Rows 3–5: 59 sc MC1.

Row 6: 59 sc MC3.

Row 7: 23 MC1, 13 CC, 23 MC1.

Row 8: 24 MC1, 11 CC, 24 MC1.

Row 9: 25 MC3, 9 CC, 25 MC3.

Row 10: 19 MC3, 7 CC, 7 MC3, 7 CC, 19 MC3.

Row 11: 20 MC1, 7 CC, 5 MC1, 7 CC, 20 MC1.

Row 12: 21 MC3, 7 CC, 3 MC3, 7 CC, 21 MC3.

Row 13: 12 MC3, 10 CC, 15 MC3, 10 CC, 12 MC3.

Row 14: 13 MC3, 10 CC, 13 MC3, 10 CC, 13 MC3.

Row 15: 14 MC4, 10 CC, 11 MC4, 10 CC, 14 MC4.

Row 16: 3 MC3, 12 CC, 29 MC3, 12 CC, 3 MC3.

Row 17: 4 MC3, 12 CC, 27 MC3, 12 CC, 4 MC3.

Row 18: 5 MC4, 12 CC, 25 MC4, 12 CC, 5 MC4.

Row 19: 4 MC4, 12 CC, 27 MC4, 12 CC, 4 MC4.

Row 20: 3 MC3, 12 CC, 29 MC3, 12 CC, 3 MC3.

Row 21: 14 MC4, 10 CC, 11 MC4, 10 CC, 14 MC4.

Row 22: 13 MC4, 10 CC, 13 MC4, 10 CC, 13 MC4.

Row 23: 12 MC4, 10 CC, 15 MC4, 10 CC, 12 MC4.

Row 24: 21 MC5, 7 CC, 3 MC5, 7 CC, 21 MC5.

Row 25: 20 MC4, 7 CC, 5 MC4, 7 CC, 20 MC4.

Row 26: 19 MC4, 7 CC, 7 MC4, 7 CC, 19 MC4.

Row 27: 25 MC5, 9 CC, 25 MC5.

Row 28: 24 MC5, 11 CC, 24 MC5.

Row 29: 23 MC4, 13 CC, 23 MC4.

Rows 30–32: 59 MC5.

Row 33: 59 MC6.

Row 34: 23 MC5, 13 CC, 23 MC5.

Row 35: 24 MC5, 11 CC, 24 MC5.

Row 36: 25 MC6, 9 CC, 25 MC6.

Row 37: 19 MC6, 7 CC, 7 MC6, 7 CC, 19 MC6.

Row 38: 20 MC5, 7 CC, 5 MC5, 7 CC, 20 MC5.

Row 39: 21 MC6, 7 CC, 3 MC6, 7 CC, 21 MC6.

Row 40: 12 MC6, 10 CC, 15 MC6, 10 CC, 12 MC6.

Row 41: 13 MC6, 10 CC, 13 MC6, 10 CC, 13 MC6.

Row 42: 14 MC7, 10 CC, 11 MC7, 10 CC, 14 MC7.

Row 43: 3 MC6, 12 CC, 29 MC6, 12 CC, 3 MC6.

Row 44: 4 MC6, 12 CC, 27 MC6, 12 CC, 4 MC6.

Row 45: 5 MC7, 12 CC, 25 MC7, 12 CC, 5 MC7.

Row 46: 4 MC7, 12 CC, 27 MC7, 12 CC, 4 MC7.

Large Wall Hanging Chart

Each square represents one single crochet stitch.

The chart is symmetrical and can be read from right to left or left to right.

Row 47: 3 MC6, 12 CC, 29 MC6, 12 CC, 3 MC6.

Row 48: 14 MC7, 10 CC, 11 MC7, 10 CC, 14 MC7.

Row 49: 13 MC7, 10 CC, 13 MC7, 10 CC, 13 MC7.

Row 50: 12 MC7, 10 CC, 15 MC7, 10 CC, 12 MC7.

Row 51: 21 MC2, 7 CC, 3 MC2, 7 CC, 21 MC2.

Row 52: 20 MC7, 7 CC, 5 MC7, 7 CC, 20 MC7.

Row 53: 19 MC7, 7 CC, 7 MC7, 7 CC, 19 MC7.

Row 54: 25 MC2, 9 CC, 25 MC2.

Row 55: 24 MC2, 11 CC, 24 MC2.

Row 56: 23 MC7, 13 CC, 23 MC7.

Rows 57–59: 59 MC2.

Row 60: 59 MC1.

Row 61: 23 MC2, 13 CC, 23 MC2.

Row 62: 24 MC2, 11 CC, 24 MC2.

Row 63: 25 MC1, 9 CC, 25 MC1.

Row 64: 19 MC1, 7 CC, 7 MC1, 7 CC, 19 MC1.

Row 65: 20 MC2, 7 CC, 5 MC2, 7 CC, 20 MC2.

Row 66: 21 MC1, 7 CC, 3 MC1, 7 CC, 21 MC1.

Row 67: 12 MC1, 10 CC, 15 MC1, 10 CC, 12 MC1.

Row 68: 13 MC1, 10 CC, 13 MC1, 10 CC, 13 MC1.

Row 69: 14 MC3, 10 CC, 11 MC3, 10 CC, 14 MC3.

Row 70: 3 MC1, 12 CC, 29 MC1, 12 CC, 3 MC1.

Row 71: 4 MC1, 12 CC, 27 MC1, 12 CC, 4 MC1.

Row 72: 5 MC3, 12 CC, 25 MC3, 12 CC, 5 MC3.

Row 73: 4 MC3, 12 CC, 27 MC3, 12 CC, 4 MC3.

Row 74: 3 MC1, 12 CC, 29 MC1, 12 CC, 3 MC1.

Row 75: 14 MC3, 10 CC, 11 MC3, 10 CC, 14 MC3.

Row 76: 13 MC3, 10 CC, 13 MC3, 10 CC, 13 MC3.

Row 77: 12 MC3, 10 CC, 15 MC3, 10 CC, 12 MC3.

Row 78: 21 MC4, 7 CC, 3 MC4, 7 CC, 21 MC4.

Row 79: 20 MC3, 7 CC, 5 MC3, 7 CC, 20 MC3.

Row 80: 19 MC3, 7 CC, 7 MC3, 7 CC, 19 MC3.

Row 81: 25 MC4, 9 CC, 25 MC4.

Row 82: 24 MC4, 11 CC, 24 MC4.

Row 83: 23 MC3, 13 CC, 23 MC3.

Rows 84–86: 59 MC4.

Row 87: 59 MC5.

Rows 88 and 89: 59 MC4.

Rows 90 and 91: 59 MC5.

Fasten off.

BOTH WALL HANGINGS

Hanging Cord

Using MC1, ch 4, sl st in first st to form a loop, ch 36 for small wall hanging or ch 48 for large wall hanging, sl st in 4th st from hook to form a loop.

Fasten off and weave in ends.

To Hang

Thread a dowel through the loops of the last row. Slide the hanging cord loops onto the ends. If the hanging cord ends slide toward the center of the wall hanging, cut a small notch at the bottom of the end of each dowel for the cord to rest in.

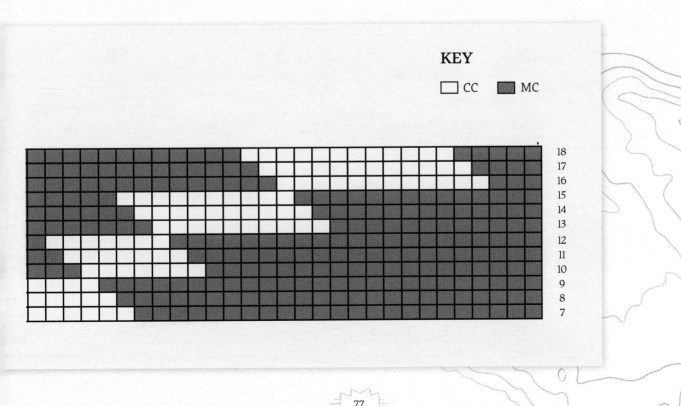

LAND OF ENCHANTMENT
Blanket & Pillow

The "Land of Enchantment" is the official nickname of the state of New Mexico, and it is truly fitting. I guarantee you will see something magical if you take a road trip in this state! Famous scenic routes through New Mexico include the Turquoise Trail between Albuquerque and Santa Fe, the High Road from Santa Fe to Taos, the Singing Road near Roswell, and the Enchanted Circle Drive through the Carson National Forest. The pace of life slows down to a leisurely walk in New Mexico so you can notice and enjoy the finer things.

Buildings with earthen adobe walls and thick wooden beams, or *vigas*, wide-open turquoise skies, and a relaxed attitude are the hallmarks of laid-back New Mexican style. Inspired by the mesas and traditional adobe architecture of New Mexico, this throw-sized blanket and matching pillows make use of a minimalist color palette. These projects are an easy introduction to tapestry crochet and use only simple double crochet stitches in just two colors.

SUPPLIES

YARN
Worsted (aran) weight in two colors

Blanket: Main Color (MC) 1,300yd (1,189m), Contrast Color (CC) 1,500yd (1,372m)

Shown in Dibe' be' iina (Sheep is Life) Navajo Nation yarn (100% Navajo Churro wool); 190yd (174m)/113g: Blanket: Gray (MC, 7 skeins) and White Heather (CC, 8 skeins); Pillow: Gray (MC, 3 skeins) and White Heather (CC, 3 skeins)

YARN ALTERNATIVES
Patons Classic Wool Worsted, Brown Sheep Lamb's Pride Worsted, Cascade 220, Knit Picks Wool of the Andes Worsted, Stylecraft Special Aran, Lily Sugar 'n Cream cotton

OTHER MATERIALS
24in (61cm) square pillow form

HOOK
4.5mm (US 7) crochet hook for blanket, 3.25mm (D/3) hook for pillow

GAUGE
Blanket: 13 sts and 8 rows = 4in (10cm) in dc

Pillow: 18 sts and 8 rows = 4in (10cm) in dc

SIZE
Blanket: 52 x 64in (132 x 163cm)

Pillow: 22½in square (57cm square)

Pattern Notes

You can choose whether to carry both yarn colors throughout the piece for ease (weaving in fewer yarn tails) or to work from a separate ball of yarn for each section of color for an ultra-clean look. To change colors, yarn over with the new color to complete the last stitch in the old color. Both colors may be carried throughout the whole blanket, or each section of color can be worked from its own ball of yarn.

BLANKET

Using MC, ch 170.

Row 1: Dc in 3rd ch from hook and all ch across, turn. (168 sts)

Rows 2–8: Ch 3 (counts as first dc), 167 dc in MC.

Rows 9–11: [7 dc CC, 42 dc MC, 7 dc CC] 3 times.

Rows 12–14: [14 dc CC, 28 dc MC, 14 dc CC] 3 times.

Rows 15–17: [21 dc CC, 14 dc MC, 21 dc CC] 3 times.

Rows 18–25: Using CC, 168 dc.

Rows 26 and 27: Using MC, 168 dc.

Rows 28–30: Using CC, 168 dc.

Rows 31–35: Using MC, 168 dc.

Rows 36–38: Using CC, 168 dc.

Rows 39 and 40: Using MC, 168 dc.

Rows 41–48: Using CC, 168 dc.

Rows 49–51: Rep Rows 15–17.

Rows 52–54: Rep Rows 12–14.

Rows 55 and 56: Rep Rows 9 and 10.

Rows 57–59: Using MC, 168 dc.

Rows 60 and 61: Rep Rows 9 and 10.

Rows 62–64: Rep Rows 12–14.

Rows 65–67: Rep Rows 15–17.

Rows 68–98: Rep Rows 18–48.

Rows 99–101: Rep Rows 15–17.

Rows 102–104: Rep Rows 12–14.

Rows 105–107: Rep Rows 9–11.

Rows 108–115: Using MC, 168 dc.

Fasten off.

Finishing

Weave in ends. Block if desired.

PILLOW FRONT/BACK

(make 2)

Using MC, ch 102.

Row 1: Dc in 3rd ch from hook and all ch across, turn. (100 sts)

Rows 2–8: Ch 3 (counts as first dc), 99 dc.

Rows 9–11: [7 dc CC, 36 dc MC, 7 dc CC] twice.

Rows 12–14: [12 dc CC, 26 dc MC, 12 dc CC] twice.

Rows 15–17: [17 dc CC, 16 dc MC, 17 dc CC] twice.

Rows 18–35: Using CC, 100 dc.

Rows 36–38: Rep Rows 15–17.

Rows 39–41: Rep Rows 12–14.

Rows 42–44: Rep Rows 9–11.

Rows 45–52: Rep Rows 2–8.

Fasten off, pull yarn tails to back of work, and knot if desired. Block to dimensions if desired.

Finishing

With WS facing out, single crochet through both layers around three sides. Turn RS out, insert the pillow form, and slip stitch across the opening. Fasten off and weave in ends.

FELTED LUMBAR PILLOW VARIATION

For a fun variation, try your hand at a wet felting technique using a washing machine to make a wool lumbar pillow that provides a perfect back support for crocheting.

Using wool yarn, follow the pattern as directed for the pillow but fasten off after Row 26. Weave in ends.

Wash in a washing machine with hot water and tumble dry. Wash with hot water again and leave wet. Block into an even rectangle, about 11 x 16in (28 x 41cm).

Sew the pillow front to the back with a sewing thread and a needle.

Fits a 12 x 18in (30.5 x 46cm) pillow form.

VALLECITO
Blanket

Vallecito Lake is nestled in a beautiful, secluded valley 8,000ft (2,438m) above sea level near my house. One of the largest bodies of water in the Four Corners area, it's breathtakingly gorgeous when the sunlight glistens over the water or when blanketed by snow in winter. Vallecito is a favorite weekend spot for my family to play in nature, and one of my favorite places to relax and crochet! The immaculate beauty of a turkey feather inspired this blanket's southwestern feather motif.

Vallecito Lake, Durango, Colorado

This intermediate tapestry crochet pattern uses double crochet stitches and five colors for eye-catching colorwork in a feathered arrow motif. Layered tassels and an ombré border bring a fun finish for a southwestern blanket that's perfect for winter gifting.

SUPPLIES

YARN

Worsted weight in five colors

Main Color (MC): 2,022yd (1,848m)

Contrast Color 1 (CC1): 400yd (366m)

Contrast Color 2 (CC2): 400yd (366m)

Contrast Color 3 (CC3): 400yd (366m)

Contrast Color 4 (CC4): 400yd (366m)

Shown in Lily Sugar 'n Cream yarn (100% cotton); 120yd (110m)/70.9g: Overcast (MC, 17 balls) and Beach Glass (CC1, 4 balls), Mod Blue (CC2, 4 balls), Teal (CC3, 4 balls), and Marine Blue (CC4, 4 balls)

HOOK

4.5mm (US 7) crochet hook

GAUGE

14 sts and 7 rows = 4in (10cm) in dc

SIZE

53 x 70in (135 x 178cm)

Pattern Notes

Wind CC yarns into small balls to make color changing easier. To change colors, yarn over with the new color halfway through the last stitch in the old color. For a smaller blanket with only one feather motif for babies or kids, skip to the border after Row 46.

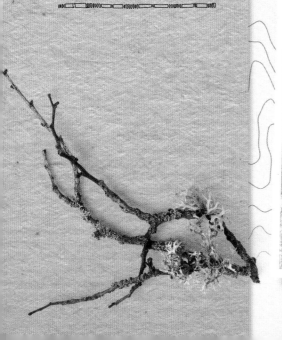

BLANKET

Using MC, ch 166.

Row 1: Dc in 3rd ch from hook and in each ch across, turn. (164 sts)

Rows 2–15: Ch 3 (does not count as dc here or throughout), 164 dc.

Row 16: Ch 3, 72 dc MC, 4 dc CC4, 12 dc MC, 4 dc CC4, 72 dc MC.

Row 17: Ch 3, 72 MC, 4 CC3, 4 CC4, 4 MC, 4 CC4, 4 CC3, 72 MC.

Row 18: Ch 3, 60 MC, 4 CC4, 8 MC, 4 CC2, 4 CC3, 4 CC4, 4 CC3, 4 CC2, 8 MC, 4 CC4, 60 MC.

Row 19: Ch 3, 60 MC, 4 CC3, 4 CC4, 4 MC, 4 CC1, 4 CC2, 4 CC3, 4 CC2, 4 CC1, 4 MC, 4 CC4, 4 CC3, 60 MC.

Row 20: Ch 3, 60 MC, 4 CC2, 4 CC3, 4 CC4, 4 MC, 4 CC1, 4 CC2, 4 CC1, 4 MC, 4 CC4, 4 CC3, 4 CC2, 60 MC.

Row 21: Ch 3, 48 MC, 4 CC4, 8 MC, 4 CC1, 4 CC2, 4 CC3, 8 MC, 4 CC1, 8 MC, 4 CC3, 4 CC2, 4 CC1, 8 MC, 4 CC4, 48 MC.

Row 22: Ch 3, 32 MC, 4 CC4, 12 MC, 4 CC3, 4 CC4, 8 MC, 4 CC1, 4 CC2, 4 MC, 4 CC4, 4 MC, 4 CC4, 4 MC, 4 CC2, 4 CC1, 8 MC, 4 CC4, 4 CC3, 12 MC, 4 CC4, 32 MC.

Row 23: Ch 3, 32 MC, 4 CC3, 4 CC4, 8 MC, 4 CC2, 4 CC3, 4 CC4, 8 MC, 4 CC1, 4 MC, 4 CC3, 4 CC4, 4 CC3, 4 MC, 4 CC1, 8 MC, 4 CC4, 4 CC3, 4 CC2, 8 MC, 4 CC4, 4 CC3, 32 MC.

Row 24: Ch 3, 32 MC, 4 CC2, 4 CC3, 4 CC4, 4 MC, 4 CC1, 4 CC2, 4 CC3, 4 MC, 4 CC4, 8 MC, 4 CC2, 4 CC3, 4 CC2, 8 MC, 4 CC4, 4 MC, 4 CC3, 4 CC2, 4 CC1, 4 MC, 4 CC4, 4 CC3, 4 CC2, 32 MC.

Row 25: Ch 3, 32 MC, 4 CC1, 4 CC2, 4 CC3, 4 CC4, 4 MC, 4 CC1, 4 CC2, 4 MC, 4 CC3, 4 CC4, 4 MC, 4 CC1, 4 CC2, 4 CC1, 4 MC, 4 CC4, 4 CC3, 4 MC, 4 CC2, 4 CC1, 4 MC, 4 CC4, 4 CC3, 4 CC2, 4 CC1, 32 MC.

Row 26: Ch 3, 36 MC, 4 CC1, 4 CC2, 4 CC3, 4 CC4, 4 MC, 4 CC1, 4 MC, 4 CC2, 4 CC3, 4 CC4, 4 MC, 4 CC1, 4 MC, 4 CC4, 4 CC3, 4 CC2, 4 MC, 4 CC1, 4 MC, 4 CC4, 4 CC3, 4 CC2, 4 CC1, 36 MC.

Row 27: Ch 3, 40 MC, 4 CC1, 4 CC2, 4 CC3, 4 CC4, 8 MC, 4 CC1, 4 CC2, 4 CC3, 4 CC4, 4 MC, 4 CC4, 4 CC3, 4 CC2, 4 CC1, 8 MC, 4 CC4, 4 CC3, 4 CC2, 4 CC1, 40 MC.

Row 28: Rep Row 26.

Row 29: Rep Row 25.

Row 30: Rep Row 24.

Row 31: Rep Row 23.

Row 32: Rep Row 22.

Row 33: Rep Row 21.

Row 34: Rep Row 20.

Row 35: Rep Row 19.

Row 36: Rep Row 18.

Row 37: Rep Row 17.

Row 38: Rep Row 16.

Rows 39–46: Rep Row 2.

Rows 47–69: Rep Rows 16–38.

Rows 70–77: Rep Row 2.

Rows 78–100: Rep Rows 16–38.

Rows 101–115: Rep Row 2.

Fasten off.

Border

Attach MC yarn to one of the short ends of the blanket, two or three stitches from the corner.

Round 1: Ch 1, sc evenly around, working 3 sc into each corner and 2 sc into each dc along ends of each row, sl st to first sc of round, turn.

Fasten off MC.

Rounds 2–4: Using CC1, ch 1, sc in each st around, working 3 sc into each corner st, sl st to first sc of round, turn.

Fasten off CC1 after Round 4.

Rounds 5–7: Using CC2, rep Rounds 2–4.

Rounds 8–10: Using CC3, rep Rounds 2–4.

Rounds 11–13: Using CC4, rep Rounds 2–4.

Fasten off and weave in all ends.

Tassels

(make 4)

For each tassel, cut 20 pieces of CC1 each 24in (61cm) long, 24 pieces of CC2 each 20in (51cm) long, 30 pieces of CC3 each 18in (46cm) long, and 32 pieces of CC4 each 12in (30.5cm) long. Cut a 14in (36cm) length of MC to use as a tie and place it horizontally on a flat surface (see Techniques: Layered Tassels). Place the CC1 pieces vertically on top of the tie, then place the CC2 pieces on top of the CC1 pieces, the CC3 pieces on top of the CC2 pieces, and the CC4 pieces on top of the CC3 pieces. Knot the tie around all pieces to fasten. Wrap the top of the tassel with a 36in (91cm) length of MC to secure. Trim the tassel as desired. Attach a tassel to each corner of the blanket using the tie ends and a tapestry needle.

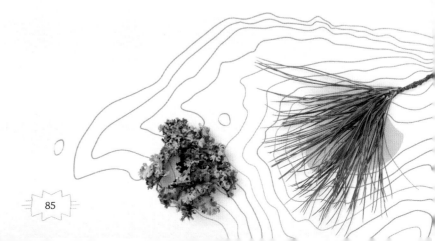

LONE MESA
Pillows & Tote

Lone Mesa in the canyonlands of Utah rises about 1,000ft (305m) above the outdoor recreation mecca town of Moab. It offers solitude and wide-open views for miles, making it the perfect place to watch a sunrise or sunset. When a late afternoon thunderstorm rolls through, the view turns dramatic. There is a beautiful variety of cacti and other desert plants and a peaceful serenity. Lone Mesa campground also hosts yearly gatherings for people with vintage Volkswagen Vanagon camper vans!

These pillows and tote bring relaxed southwest style to your home or wardrobe. A handful of yarn scraps or a cake of self-striping yarn creates impressive colorwork that's much easier than it looks! Use the leftover yarn from your Modern Bohemian Blanket or Canyon Moon Blanket to make a coordinating pillow or tote. Use worsted weight yarn and a relatively small hook to create a tight, sturdy fabric to prevent the tote from stretching during use. Fringe accents and leather straps elevate the look.

SUPPLIES

YARN

Worsted (aran) weight yarn

Small pillow: MC 500yd (457m) (about 31yd/28m of each of 16 colors), CC 150yd (137m)

Large pillow: MC 600yd (549m), CC 150yd (137m) (about 12.5yd/11.4m of each of 12 colors)

Tote: MC 685yd (626m), CC 400yd (366m)

Pillows shown in Shepherd's Lamb Churro Yarn (100% certified organic churro wool); 225yd (206m)/114g skein: White (MC, 3 skeins), Green Heather (CC, 1 skein), Green Chile (CC, 1 skein), Aspen (CC, 1 skein), Brown Heather (CC, 1 skein), Red Heather (CC, 1 skein), Chile Colorado (CC 1 skein), Iron Springs (CC, 1 skein), Calabasa (CC, 1 skein), Yellow Heather (CC, 1 skein), Tierra Amarilla (CC, 1 skein), Blue Heather (CC, 1 skein), Viento (CC, 1 skein), Guadalupe (CC, 1 skein), Cielo (CC, 1 skein); listed quantities are enough to make both the small and large pillows

Tote shown in Four Corners Yarns High Desert Heathered (50% Navajo Churro wool, 50% merino wool); 200yd (183m)/105g: Undyed Gray (MC, 4 skeins), Smokey Lavender (1 skein), Brick (1 skein), Rust (1 skein), Mustard (1 skein), Goldenseal (1 skein), Olive (1 skein), Fern (1 skein), Aqua (1 skein), Dragonfly (1 skein), Teal (1 skein), Aloe (1 skein), and Violet (1 skein)

OTHER MATERIALS

14 x 18in (36 x 46cm) pillow form for small pillow, 18in (46cm) square pillow form for large pillow, 68in (173cm) of ¾in (2cm)-wide strap and 8 screw-in rivets (Chicago screws) for the tote

HOOK

2.75mm (C/2) crochet hook

GAUGE

19 sts and 10 rows = 4in (10cm) in dc

SIZE

Small pillow: 13 x 17in (33 x 43cm) to fit a 14 x 18in (36 x 46cm) pillow form

Large pillow: 17in (43cm) square to fit an 18in (46cm) square pillow form

Tote: 18in (46cm) square, 2½in (6cm) deep

Pattern Notes

The front and back of each pillow or tote square are identical. The tote side gusset is made from several rounds of single crochet around one square, then the second square is joined. This is a scrap yarn-friendly project; you can substitute DK weight yarn to make a 16in (41cm) square pillow or 12 by 16in (30.5 by 41cm) lumbar pillow. The CC yarn is changed every row from Row 11 to Row 22, then the color order is reversed for Rows 23 to 33. Both MC and CC yarns can be carried across each row; crochet over the color not in use. To change colors, yarn over with the new color halfway through your last stitch in the old color. The CC yarn can be cut and knotted after each row and knots hidden inside the pillow.

SMALL PILLOW

Use solid white as the CC and colorful yarns or a self-striping yarn as the MC. Attach a new strand of MC yarn to begin each row, leaving an 8in (20cm) yarn tail to create a fringe. Cut the yarn and fasten off after each row, leaving an 8in (20cm) yarn tail. Do not turn the work.

Small Pillow Rectangle

(make 2)

Using MC, ch 83.

Row 1: Dc in 3rd ch from hook and each ch across, turn. (81 dc)

Rows 2–4: Ch 3 (counts as first st here and throughout), 80 dc.

Rows 5–16: Ch 3, dc in each st across, changing colors from MC to CC and back according to written Color Change Instructions or chart.

Row 17: Rep Row 15.

Row 18: Rep Row 14.

Row 19: Rep Row 13.

Row 20: Rep Row 12.

Row 21: Rep Row 11.

Row 22: Rep Row 10.

Row 23: Rep Row 9.

Row 24: Rep Row 8.

Row 25: Rep Row 7.

Row 26: Rep Row 6.

Row 27: Rep Row 5.

Rows 28–31: Using MC, ch 3, 80 dc.

Color Change Instructions

Row 5: 33 MC, 3 CC, 9 MC, 3 CC, 33 MC.

Row 6: 33 MC, 6 CC, 3 MC, 6 CC, 33 MC.

Row 7: 24 MC, 3 CC, 6 MC, 15 CC, 6 MC, 3 CC, 24 MC.

Row 8: 24 MC, 6 CC, 3 MC, 15 CC, 3 MC, 6 CC, 24 MC.

Row 9: 24 MC, [9 CC, 3 MC] twice, 9 CC, 24 MC.

Row 10: 15 MC, [3 CC, 6 MC, 9 CC, 6 MC] twice, 3 CC, 15 MC.

Row 11: 6 MC, 3 CC, [6 MC, 6 CC] twice, [3 MC, 3 CC] twice, 3 MC, [6 CC, 6 MC] twice, 3 CC, 6 MC.

Row 12: 6 MC, 6 CC, 3 MC, 9 CC, 6 MC, 3 CC, 3 MC, 9 CC, 3 MC, 3 CC, 6 MC, 9 CC, 3 MC, 6 CC, 6 MC.

Row 13: 6 MC, 18 CC, 3 MC, 3 CC, 6 MC, 9 CC, 6 MC, 3 CC, 3 MC, 18 CC, 6 MC.

Row 14: 6 MC, 9 CC, [3 MC, 6 CC] twice, 3 MC, 9 CC, 3 MC, [6 CC, 3 MC] twice, 9 CC, 6 MC.

Row 15: 9 MC, [9 CC, 3 MC, 3 CC, 3 MC] 3 times, 9 CC, 9 MC.

Row 16: 12 MC, 9 CC, 6 MC, 12 CC, 3 MC, 12 CC, 6 MC, 9 CC, 12 MC.

Finishing Small Pillow

Pull all yarn tails to the WS and knot if desired. Block to dimensions if desired.

With the RS of the pillow front and back facing out, work single crochet through both layers evenly across top edge and bottom edge of pillow. Insert the pillow form and tie the yarn ends from the front and back of pillow together row by row in a double knot to close the side openings. Tie the knotted ends from two rows (four yarn tails total) in an overhand knot. Trim yarn tails evenly.

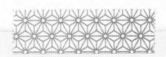

Chart

Each square of the chart represents three double crochet stitches in one row.
The chart is symmetrical and can be read from right to left or left to right.

KEY

 3 MC sts   ▨ 3 CC sts

Large pillow or tote row

Small pillow row

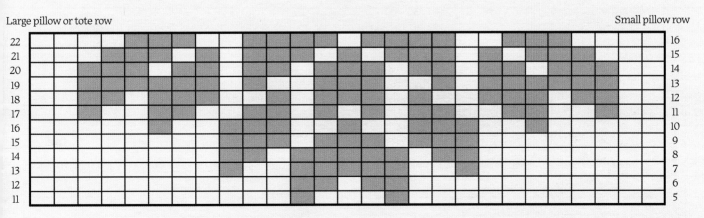

LARGE PILLOW OR TOTE SQUARE

(make 2)

Using MC, ch 83.

Row 1: Dc in 3rd ch from hook and each ch across, turn. (81 dc)

Rows 2–10: Ch 3 (counts as first st here and throughout), 80 dc, turn.

Rows 11–22: Ch 3, dc in each st across, changing colors from MC to CC and back according to written Color Change Instructions or chart, turn.

Row 23: Rep Row 21.

Row 24: Rep Row 20.

Row 25: Rep Row 19.

Row 26: Rep Row 18.

Row 27: Rep Row 17.

Row 28: Rep Row 16.

Row 29: Rep Row 15.

Row 30: Rep Row 14.

Row 31: Rep Row 13.

Row 32: Rep Row 12.

Row 33: Rep Row 11.

Rows 34–43: Using MC, ch 3, 80 dc, turn. Do not fasten off.

Color Change Instructions

Row 11: 33 MC, 3 CC, 9 MC, 3 CC, 33 MC.

Row 12: 33 MC, 6 CC, 3 MC, 6 CC, 33 MC.

Row 13: 24 MC, 3 CC, 6 MC, 15 CC, 6 MC, 3 CC, 24 MC.

Row 14: 24 MC, 6 CC, 3 MC, 15 CC, 3 MC, 6 CC, 24 MC.

Row 15: 24 MC, [9 CC, 3 MC] twice, 9 CC, 24 MC.

Row 16: 15 MC, [3 CC, 6 MC, 9 CC, 6 MC] twice, 3 CC, 15 MC.

Row 17: 6 MC, 3 CC, [6 MC, 6 CC] twice, [3 MC, 3 CC] twice, 3 MC, [6 CC, 6 MC] twice, 3 CC, 6 MC.

Row 18: 6 MC, 6 CC, 3 MC, 9 CC, 6 MC, 3 CC, 3 MC, 9 CC, 3 MC, 3 CC, 6 MC, 9 CC, 3 MC, 6 CC, 6 MC.

Row 19: 6 MC, 18 CC, 3 MC, 3 CC, 6 MC, 9 CC, 6 MC, 3 CC, 3 MC, 18 CC, 6 MC.

Row 20: 6 MC, 9 CC, [3 MC, 6 CC] twice, 3 MC, 9 CC, 3 MC, [6 CC, 3 MC] twice, 9 CC, 6 MC.

Row 21: 9 MC, [9 CC, 3 MC, 3 CC, 3 MC] 3 times, 9 CC, 9 MC.

Row 22: 12 MC, 9 CC, 6 MC, 12 CC, 3 MC, 12 CC, 6 MC, 9 CC, 12 MC.

Border (Large Pillow and Tote Squares Only)

Round 1: Ch 1, turn, work sc evenly around all edges of square, working 3 sc into each corner and 2 sc into each dc at the end of each row, join with sl st in first sc.

Fasten off.

Finishing Large Pillow

Pull all yarn tails to WS and knot if desired. Block to dimensions if desired.

With the RS of the pillow front and back facing out, work single crochet through both layers evenly around three edges of the pillow. Insert the pillow form and work single crochet evenly along the last side to close the opening. Weave in all ends.

Finishing Tote

Weave in ends. Block to dimensions if desired.

Side Gusset

Row 1: Using CC and with RS of a square facing down, attach yarn at left corner of top of square leaving a 12in (30.5cm) tail, ch 1, work sc in BLO of border evenly around 3 edges (A), working 1 sc in BLO into each corner, fasten off leaving a 12in (30.5cm) tail, do not turn. (253 sts)

Row 2: Attach CC yarn to first st of Row 1 leaving a 12in (30.5cm) tail, ch 1 (does not count as st), 1 sc in BLO of each st, working 1 sc in BLO in each corner, fasten off leaving a 12in (30.5cm) tail, do not turn.

Rows 3–11: Rep Row 2. (B)

Attach Second Square

Row 1: Attach CC yarn leaving a 12in (30.5cm) tail, 1 sc through BLO of Row 11 and BLO of each st of the border round of the second square evenly around 3 sides, fasten off leaving a 12in (30.5cm) tail. (C)

Trim all yarn ends evenly.

Attach Straps

Cut two 34in (86cm) lengths of leather, faux leather, or other strap material. Punch two holes in the end of each strap piece using a hole punch, skewer, awl, or pocketknife. Attach the straps to the tote using screw-in rivets or sew them to the tote with yarn and a needle.

WIND RIVER
Weighted Blanket

The source of the Wind River is high in Rocky Mountain National Park at the Continental Divide, which separates the watersheds that flow into the Pacific and Atlantic Oceans. The river flows through cold, windy alpine tundra, down through protected groves of aspen, spruce, and pine, and across wildflower-covered meadows before joining other rivers on its meandering descent to the ocean.

*Wind River,
Rocky Mountain National Park*

Let these wild natural landscapes inspire a color palette to bring fresh mountain style to your living room or bedroom. Super bulky cotton yarn gives this blanket a soothing, hefty, but breathable weight. When made with the recommended Hoooked Zpagetti eco-friendly 100% recycled fiber yarn, this blanket weighs 18lb (8kg). Relax under its calming weight as you crochet, or feel free to use lighter weight yarn to make a more traditional blanket. Use a smaller hook to create a sturdy rug (above) for your kitchen or entryway.

SUPPLIES

YARN

Super bulky (super chunky) weight in five colors

Main Color (MC): 524yd (479m)

Contrast Color 1 (CC1): 524yd (479m)

Contrast Color 2 (CC2): 393yd (359m)

Contrast Color 3 (CC3): 393yd (359m)

Contrast Color 4 (CC4): 131yd (120m)

Shown in Hoooked Zpagetti (100% recycled fibers); 131yd (120m)/600g: Bordeaux Faded (MC, 4 balls), Beige Desert (CC1, 4 balls), Dried Herb (CC2, 3 balls), Autumn Mood (CC3, 3 balls), Salted Caramel (CC4, 1 ball)

YARN ALTERNATIVES

Paintbox Yarns Recycled T-Shirt, Moda Vera Craft Tee, Hoooked RibbonXL, Darn Good Yarn Cotton T-Shirt, Wool and the Gang Mixtape, Knit Picks Mighty Stitch Super Bulky

HOOK

11.5mm (P/16) crochet hook

GAUGE

6 sts and 6.5 rows = 4in (10cm) in sc

SIZE

54 x 70in (137 x 178cm)

Pattern Notes

This blanket is worked in tapestry crochet, in which each section of color is worked from a small ball or bobbin of yarn. To change colors, work in the old color up to last yarn over, then yarn over with the new color to complete the stitch. To make changing colors easier, separate the yarn into smaller balls before beginning. You will need three small balls each of MC and CC4 and four small balls each of CC1, CC2, and CC3. You can work the color changes from either the written instructions or the chart.

BLANKET

Beginning Stripes

Using MC, ch 79.

Row 1: Sc in 2nd ch from hook and each ch across, turn. (78 sts)

Rows 2–13: Ch 1 (does not count as a st), 78 sc.

Row 14: Using CC1, rep Row 2.

Rows 15 and 16: Using CC3, rep Row 2.

Row 17: Using CC4, rep Row 2.

Rows 18 and 19: Using CC3, rep Row 2.

Row 20: Using CC1, rep Row 2.

Rows 21–23: Using MC, rep Row 2.

Colorwork Section

Row 24: Ch 1, [5 sc CC1, 29 sc MC, 5 sc CC1] twice, turn.

Row 25: Ch 1, [4 sc CC1, 31 sc MC, 4 sc CC1] twice, turn.

Row 26: Ch 1, [3 sc CC1, 33 sc MC, 3 sc CC1] twice, turn.

Row 27: Ch 1, [12 sc CC1, 15 sc MC, 12 sc CC1] twice, turn.

Row 28: Ch 1, [11 sc CC1, 17 sc MC, 11 sc CC1] twice, turn.

Row 29: Ch 1, [10 sc CC1, 19 sc MC, 10 sc CC1] twice, turn.

Row 30: Ch 1, [7 sc CC2, 10 sc CC1, 5 sc MC, 10 sc CC1, 7 sc CC2] twice, turn.

Row 31: Ch 1, [6 sc CC2, 10 sc CC1, 7 sc MC, 10 sc CC1, 6 sc CC2] twice, turn.

Row 32: Ch 1, [5 sc CC2, 10 sc CC1, 9 sc MC, 10 sc CC1, 5 sc CC2] twice, turn.

Row 33: Ch 1, [4 sc CC3, 7 sc CC2, 17 sc CC1, 7 sc CC2, 4 sc CC3] twice, turn.

Row 34: Ch 1, [3 sc CC3, 7 sc CC2, 19 sc CC1, 7 sc CC2, 3 sc CC3] twice, turn.

Row 35: Ch 1, [2 sc CC3, 7 sc CC2, 21 sc CC1, 7 sc CC2, 2 sc CC3] twice, turn.

Row 36: Ch 1, [8 sc CC3, 10 sc CC2, 3 sc CC1, 10 sc CC2, 8 sc CC3] twice, turn.

Row 37: Ch 1, [7 sc CC3, 10 sc CC2, 5 sc CC1, 10 sc CC2, 7 sc CC3] twice, turn.

Row 38: Ch 1, [6 sc CC3, 10 sc CC2, 7 sc CC1, 10 sc CC2, 6 sc CC3] twice, turn.

Row 39: Ch 1, [4 sc CC4, 11 sc CC3, 9 sc CC2, 11 sc CC3, 4 sc CC4] twice, turn.

Row 40: Ch 1, [3 sc CC4, 11 sc CC3, 11 sc CC2, 11 sc CC3, 3 sc CC4] twice, turn.

Row 41: Ch 1, [2 sc CC4, 11 sc CC3, 13 sc CC2, 11 sc CC3, 2 sc CC4] twice, turn.

Row 42: Rep Row 40.

Row 43: Rep Row 39.

Row 44: Rep Row 38.

Row 45: Rep Row 37.

Row 46: Rep Row 36.

Row 47: Rep Row 35.

Row 48: Rep Row 34.

Row 49: Rep Row 33.

Row 50: Rep Row 32.

Row 51: Rep Row 31.

Row 52: Rep Row 30.

Row 53: Rep Row 29.

Row 54: Rep Row 28.

Row 55: Rep Row 27.

Row 56: Rep Row 26.

Row 57: Rep Row 25.

Rows 58–91: Rep Rows 24–57.

Row 92: Rep Row 24.

Ending Stripes

Rows 93–95: Using MC, rep Row 2.

Row 96: Using CC1, rep Row 2.

Rows 97 and 98: Using CC3, rep Row 2.

Row 99: Using CC4, rep Row 2.

Rows 100 and 101: Using CC3, rep Row 2.

Row 102: Using CC1, rep Row 2.

Rows 103–115: Using MC, rep Row 2.

Fasten off.

Finishing

Weave in all ends with a large tapestry needle or small crochet hook.

Block to dimensions if desired.

RUG VARIATION

Use bulky or super bulky weight yarn and a 6.5mm (K/10½) hook to make a rug. You will need 393yd (359m) of MC, 262yd (240m) of CC1 and CC2, 131yd (120m) of CC3, and 65yd (60m) of CC4.

Shown in Hoooked RibbonXL yarn (100% recycled fibers); 131yd (120m)/250g in Stone Gray (MC, 3 skeins), Sandy Ecru (CC1, 2 skeins), Riverside Jeans (CC2, 2 skeins), Caramel Brown (CC3, 1 skein), and Harvest Ochre (CC4, 1 skein).

Finished dimensions 33 x 45in (84 x 114cm).

Chart

Each square represents one single crochet stitch. The chart is symmetrical and can be read from right to left or left to right.

The pattern repeat is 39 stitches wide. The chart repeats twice per row for a total of 78 stitches per row. After Row 57, start again at Row 24.

KEY

⊙ MC

☐ CC1

◼ CC2

⊡ CC3

✚ CC4

▣ Pattern rep

CANYON MOON
Blanket

A new southwestern version of the classic Wedding Ring blanket. The Wedding Ring quilt became popular in the 1920s, but the motif of interlocking rings goes back at least as far as the fourth century when it was used to decorate Roman cups. In Native American traditions, circles are symbolic of the sun, the moon, the cycles of the seasons, the cycle of life to death to rebirth, family ties, closeness, and protection, holding that which cannot be broken. Throughout the years, this motif has also been called Coiled Rattlesnake, Endless Chain, Around the World, and Friendship Knot.

The Wedding Ring blanket thread weaves through my family history, too. One of my oldest possessions is a worn cotton single Wedding Ring quilt, stitched by a female relative and made buttery soft by time. The handwork of my ancestors inspires me to carry on the family tradition in my own way. Use neutral colors for an heirloom-quality wedding gift or choose bold brights for a stunningly hypnotic blanket for yourself or a friend.

SUPPLIES

YARN
DK weight or fine weight held doubled

Main Color (MC): 2,733yd (2,499m)

Contrast Color (CC): 1,035yd (946m)

Shown in Hobbii Cotton Kings Sultan Deluxe (100% cotton); 1,093yd (1,000m)/250g cake: Baltic Amber (MC, 2 cakes), Mojave Azurite (MC, 2 cakes), and Oppenheimer Blue (MC, ½ of each of 2 cakes), and Hobbii Baby Cotton Organic Midi (100% organic cotton); 115yd (105m)/50g ball: Titanium (CC, 9 balls); fine weight MC yarn was held doubled in the sample to match the DK weight of the CC yarn

YARN ALTERNATIVES
Red Heart It's A Wrap, Schoppel-Wolle Zauberball Cotton, Rico Creative Cotton Dégradé, Cotton Kings Twirls, Lion Brand Mandala

HOOK
3.75mm (F/5) crochet hook

GAUGE
21 sts and 9 rows in 4in (10cm) in dc

SIZE
48 x 60in (122 x 152cm)

Pattern Notes

Both the MC and CC yarn are carried throughout the whole blanket, making color changes easy. Crochet over the color you are not using by laying it on top of the stitches of the row below, and crochet around it to hide it. Change colors by yarning over with the new color as the last yarn over of the last stitch in the old color. Each pattern repeat is 42 stitches across and 18 rows tall.

Gradient Yarn Cakes For Tapestry Crochet

Gradient yarns provide an easy way to add dramatic color to a project without changing yarns frequently. You can see them used here in the Canyon Moon Blanket and in the Globe Trekker Throw. Fine weight yarn cakes can be used held doubled—crocheting with two strands of yarn held together as one. This creates very smooth color transitions because the gradients of the two matching yarn cakes differ slightly. Start using the gradient yarn from the inside of the cake to the outside or vice versa to suit your preferred color order. Match the weight of the contrast color yarn to the doubled gradient yarns as closely as possible.

BLANKET

Using CC, ch 253.

Row 1: Sc in 2nd loop from hook and all ch across, turn. (252 sts)

Color Change Instructions

Rows 2–130: Ch 3 (does not count as a st), dc in each st across, changing colors from MC to CC and back as directed in the Color Change Instructions or chart.

Row 2: Ch 3, [20 MC, 2 CC, 20 MC] 6 times.

Rows 3 and 4: Rep Row 2.

Row 5: Ch 3, [18 MC, 6 CC, 18 MC] 6 times.

Row 6: Ch 3, [18 MC, 2 CC, 2 MC, 2 CC, 18 MC] 6 times.

Row 7: Ch 3, [14 MC, 6 CC, 2 MC, 6 CC, 14 MC] 6 times.

Row 8: Ch 3, [14 MC, 2 CC, 10 MC, 2 CC, 14 MC] 6 times.

Row 9: Ch 3, [10 MC, 6 CC, 10 MC, 6 CC, 10 MC] 6 times.

Row 10: Ch 3, [8 MC, 4 CC, 18 MC, 4 CC, 8 MC] 6 times.

Row 11: Ch 3, [4 MC, 6 CC, 22 MC, 6 CC, 4 MC] 6 times.

Row 12: Ch 3, [6 CC, 30 MC, 6 CC] 6 times.

Row 13: Rep Row 11.

Row 14: Rep Row 10.

Row 15: Rep Row 9.

Row 16: Rep Row 8.

Row 17: Rep Row 7.

Row 18: Rep Row 6.

Row 19: Rep Row 5.

Rows 20–127: Rep Rows 2-19 six more times.

Rows 128–130: Rep Row 2.

Row 131: Using CC, ch 1, 252 sc.

Border

Preparation Rows (optional): Using CC, sc evenly along each long edge of the blanket, working 2 sc into each dc at the end of each row.

Rounds 1–3: Ch 1, sc in each st around blanket, working 3 sc into each corner st, sl st to first sc.

Fasten off and weave in ends.

Chart

Each square of the chart represents two double crochet stitches.

The chart is symmetrical and can be read from right to left or left to right.

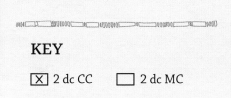

KEY

☒ 2 dc CC   ☐ 2 dc MC

GLOBE TREKKER
Throw

This throw is inspired by the ikat dyeing and weaving traditions in Central and Southeast Asia, India, Africa, and Latin America, but it's right at home here in the American southwest. Ikat means "to tie" or "to bind" in Indonesia, and ikat cloth is traditionally made of silk. The threads are bound with ribbon to create a resist and are dyed in patterns before they are warped on the weaving loom. Sometimes both the warp and weft threads are dyed before weaving, creating a cloth called double ikat. Ikat weaving is highly prized because it is laborious and difficult work.

The traditional feathered edge look to ikat designs is recreated here in blocks of double crochet stitches. Every other row is the same as the one below it, making this blanket a relaxing project to stitch for yourself or a loved one. Let the open-air textile markets of the world be your color inspiration as you select your yarn. The more colorful, the better! Double-layered tassels add exotic flair to complete the boho look.

SUPPLIES

YARN
DK weight or fine weight held doubled

Main Color (MC): 2,100yd (1,920m)

Contrast Color (CC): 1,150yd (1,052m) for blanket plus 460yd (421m) for border and 100yd (91m) for tassels

Shown in Hobbii Cotton Kings Sultan Deluxe (100% cotton); 1,093yd (1,000m)/250g cake: Baltic Amber (MC, 2 cakes), Blue Moon (MC, 2 cakes), and Imperial Purple (MC, 2 cakes), and Hobbii Baby Cotton Organic Midi (100% organic cotton); 115yd (105m)/50g ball: Titanium (CC, 10 balls for blanket plus 4 balls for border and 1 ball for tassels); fine weight MC yarn was held doubled in the sample to match the DK weight of the CC yarn

YARN ALTERNATIVES
Red Heart It's A Wrap, Schoppel-Wolle Zauberball Cotton, Rico Creative Cotton Dégradé, Cotton Kings Twirls, Lion Brand Mandala

HOOK
3.75mm (F/5) crochet hook for blanket, 2.75mm (C/2) hook for border

GAUGE
21 sts and 9 rows = 4in (10cm) in dc

SIZE
44 x 64in (112 x 163cm)

Pattern Notes

A self-striping yarn and a contrast yarn are both carried throughout the whole throw, making color changes easy. You can substitute yarn scraps for the self-striping yarn to turn this project into a stash buster. Crochet over the color you are not using by laying it on top of the row of stitches below, and crochet around it to hide it. Change colors by yarning over with the new color as the last yarn over of the last stitch in the old color. Each pattern repeat is 54 stitches across.

THROW

Using CC, ch 220.

Row 1: Sc in 2nd ch from hook and all ch across, turn. (219 sts)

Row 2: Attach MC, ch 3 (does not count as st here or throughout), [9 dc MC, 6 dc CC, 27 dc MC, 6 dc CC, 6 dc MC] 4 times, 3 dc MC, turn. (219 dc)

Rows 3–7: Rep Row 2.

Rows 8–11: Ch 2, [3 dc CC, 9 dc MC, 6 dc CC, 21 dc MC, 6 dc CC, 9 dc MC] 4 times, 3 dc CC, turn.

Rows 12 and 13: [3 dc CC, 12 dc MC, 6 dc CC, 15 dc MC, 6 dc CC, 12 dc MC] 4 times, 3 dc CC, turn.

Rows 14 and 15: [3 CC, 15 MC, 6 CC, 9 MC, 6 CC, 15 MC] 4 times, 3 CC, turn.

Rows 16 and 17: [6 CC, 15 MC, 6 CC, 3 MC, 6 CC, 15 MC, 3 CC] 4 times, 3 CC, turn.

Rows 18 and 19: [3 MC, 6 CC, 15 MC, 3 CC, 3 MC, 3 CC, 15 MC, 6 CC] 4 times, 3 MC, turn.

Rows 20 and 21: [6 MC, 6 CC, 12 MC, 9 CC, 12 MC, 6 CC, 3 MC] 4 times, 3 MC, turn.

Rows 22 and 23: [9 MC, 3 CC, 15 MC, 3 CC, 15 MC, 3 CC, 6 MC] 4 times, 3 MC, turn.

Rows 24 and 25: [9 MC, 6 CC, 12 MC, 3 CC, 12 MC, 6 CC, 6 MC] 4 times, 3 MC, turn.

Rows 26 and 27: [12 MC, 6 CC, 21 MC, 6 CC, 9 MC] 4 times, 3 MC, turn.

Rows 28 and 29: [3 CC, 12 MC, 3 CC, 21 MC, 3 CC, 12 MC] 4 times, 3 CC, turn.

Rows 30 and 31: [3 CC, 12 MC, 6 CC, 15 MC, 6 CC, 12 MC] 4 times, 3 CC, turn.

Rows 32 and 33: [6 CC, 12 MC, 3 CC, 15 MC, 3 CC, 12 MC, 3 CC] 4 times, 3 CC, turn.

Rows 34 and 35: [6 CC, 12 MC, 6 CC, 9 MC, 6 CC, 12 MC, 3 CC] 4 times, 3 CC, turn.

Rows 36 and 37: [3 MC, 6 CC, 12 MC, 6 CC, 3 MC, 6 CC, 12 MC, 6 CC] 4 times, 3 MC, turn.

Rows 38 and 39: [3 MC, 9 CC, 12 MC, 3 CC, 3 MC, 3 CC, 12 MC, 9 CC] 4 times, 3 MC, turn.

Rows 40 and 41: [6 MC, 9 CC, 9 MC, 9 CC, 9 MC, 9 CC, 3 MC] 4 times, 3 MC, turn.

Rows 42–45: [9 MC, 9 CC, 9 MC, 3 CC, 9 MC, 9 CC, 6 MC] 4 times, 3 MC, turn.

Rows 46–53: [12 MC, 9 CC, 15 MC, 9 CC, 9 MC] 4 times, 3 MC, turn.

Rows 54–57: [9 MC, 9 CC, 21 MC, 9 CC, 6 MC] 4 times, 3 MC, turn.

Rows 58 and 59: [6 MC, 9 CC, 27 MC, 9 CC, 3 MC] 4 times, 3 MC, turn.

Rows 60 and 61: [3 MC, 9 CC, 15 MC, 3 CC, 15 MC, 9 CC] 4 times, 3 MC, turn.

Rows 62 and 63: [3 MC, 6 CC, 18 MC, 3 CC, 18 MC, 6 CC] 4 times, 3 MC, turn.

Rows 64 and 65: [6 CC, 18 MC, 9 CC, 18 MC, 3 CC] 4 times, 3 CC, turn.

Rows 66 and 67: [6 CC, 15 MC, 6 CC, 3 MC, 6 CC, 15 MC, 3 CC] 4 times, 3 CC, turn.

Rows 68 and 69: [3 CC, 15 MC, 6 CC, 9 MC, 6 CC, 15 MC] 4 times, 3 CC, turn.

Rows 70 and 71: [3 CC, 9 MC, 9 CC, 15 MC, 9 CC, 9 MC] 4 times, 3 CC, turn.

Rows 72 and 73: [6 MC, 9 CC, 27 MC, 9 CC, 3 MC] 4 times, 3 MC, turn.

Rows 74 and 75: Rep Rows 70 and 71.

Rows 76 and 77: Rep Rows 68 and 69.

Rows 78 and 79: Rep Rows 66 and 67.

Rows 80 and 81: Rep Rows 64 and 65.

Rows 82 and 83: Rep Rows 62 and 63.

Rows 84 and 85: Rep Rows 60 and 61.

Rows 86 and 87: Rep Rows 58 and 59.

Rows 88–91: Rep Row 54.

Rows 92–99: Rep Row 46.

Rows 100–103: Rep Row 42.

Rows 104 and 105: Rep Rows 40 and 41.

Rows 106 and 107: Rep Rows 38 and 39.

Rows 108 and 109: Rep Rows 36 and 37.

Rows 110 and 111: Rep Rows 34 and 35.

Rows 112 and 113: Rep Rows 32 and 33.

Rows 114 and 115: Rep Rows 30 and 31.

Rows 116 and 117: Rep Rows 28 and 29.

Rows 118 and 119: Rep Rows 26 and 27.

Rows 120 and 121: Rep Rows 24 and 25.

Rows 122 and 123: Rep Rows 22 and 23.

Rows 124 and 125: Rep Rows 20 and 21.

Rows 126 and 127: Rep Rows 18 and 19.

Rows 128 and 129: Rep Rows 16 and 17.

Rows 130 and 131: Rep Rows 14 and 15.

Rows 132 and 133: Rep Rows 12 and 13.

Rows 134–137: Rep Row 8.

Rows 138 to 143: Rep Row 2.

Fasten off.

Border

Finish your blanket with a border of eight rounds of single crochet using CC yarn and a crochet hook 1mm smaller than the hook used for the rest of the blanket. If you used a 3.75mm (F/5) hook for the blanket, use a 2.75mm (C/2) hook for the border. This helps keep the border edge straight.

Round 1: Attach yarn with a sl st to top right edge of one short end of blanket 2 or 3 stitches from the corner, ch 1, sc evenly around, working 3 sc into each corner and 2 sc into each dc along end of each row, sl st to first sc.

Rounds 2–8: Ch 1, sc in each st around, working 3 sc in each corner st.

Fasten off and weave in all ends.

Tassels

(make 4)

Use CC yarn or any yarn you like to make the double-layered tassels (see Techniques: Layered Tassels). Cut 24 pieces each 19in (48cm) long. Cut 28 pieces each 12in (30.5cm) long. Cut one 24in (61cm) length to wrap the tassel. Cut one 14in (36cm) length to use as a tie and place it horizontally on a flat surface. Place the 19in (48cm) pieces vertically on top of the tie, then place the 12in (30.5cm) pieces on top. Tie the tie around all pieces to fasten. Wrap around the top of the tassel with the 24in (61cm) length to secure. Hide the end of the wrap yarn down inside the tassel using a yarn needle. Trim the top tassel layer to 5in (13cm) and the bottom tassel layer to 7in (18cm) or as desired. Attach a tassel to each corner of the blanket with a yarn needle and the tie ends.

Chart

Each square represents three double crochet stitches and two rows.

Read all odd-numbered (RS) rows from right to left and all even-numbered (WS) rows from left to right.

Work the chart four times per row.

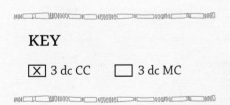

KEY

[X] 3 dc CC   [ ] 3 dc MC

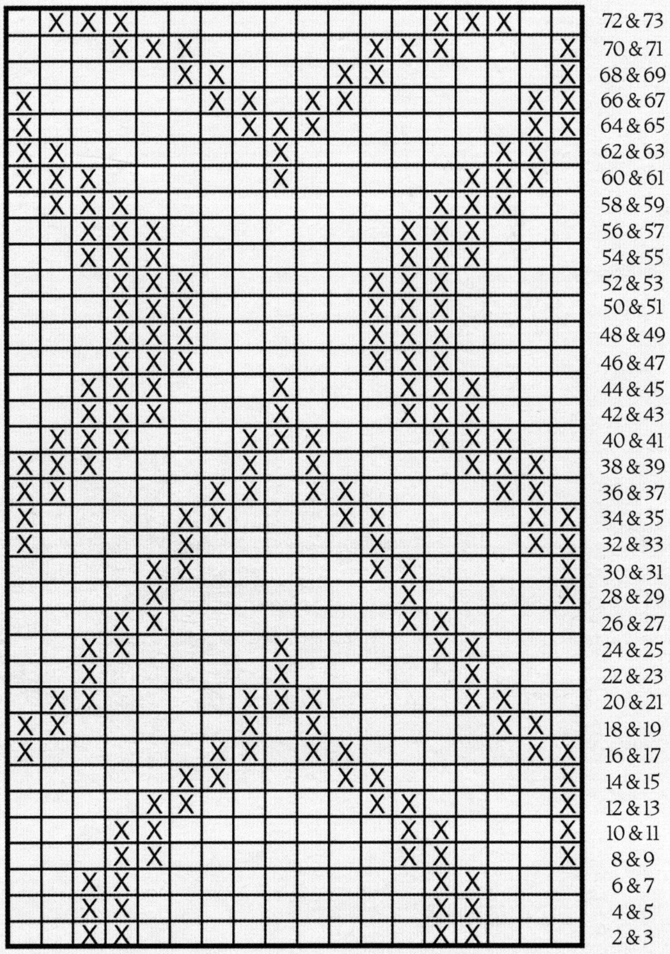

72 & 73
70 & 71
68 & 69
66 & 67
64 & 65
62 & 63
60 & 61
58 & 59
56 & 57
54 & 55
52 & 53
50 & 51
48 & 49
46 & 47
44 & 45
42 & 43
40 & 41
38 & 39
36 & 37
34 & 35
32 & 33
30 & 31
28 & 29
26 & 27
24 & 25
22 & 23
20 & 21
18 & 19
16 & 17
14 & 15
12 & 13
10 & 11
8 & 9
6 & 7
4 & 5
2 & 3

TECHNIQUES

Crochet is an art form with endless possibilities, even using only the simplest of stitches. With every stitch you make, you expand your skills and hone your techniques. One of the beautiful things about crochet is that it can always be unraveled for a fresh beginning. Don't worry if you don't get the hang of the techniques presented here on the first try. Patience and practice are the keys to crochet happiness.

In this section, you'll find instructions for the basic crochet stitches, as well as for the special stitches used in this book. Abbreviations and crochet terms are listed for your reference. You'll also find tips for creating a smooth, flat border on your projects. Borders are a great way to create clean, straight edges on crochet blankets and squares. Feel free to mix and match the borders for your projects to suit your fancy, or to omit the border altogether!

Adding fringes and tassels is an easy way to turn any project into a bohemian masterpiece. They can transform a simple project into a visually stunning piece with color, texture, and beautiful movement. This section covers several types of fringes and how to add them to your projects as well as step-by-step guidance on how to make colorful layered tassels.

Tapestry crochet techniques are explained, along with tips and tricks for crocheting with many colors. Using multiple colors in a project is truly joyful, but it does increase the risk of yarn tangles. You'll find techniques covered here to ease this problem, even when you're working with five or more colors in a single row.

Mosaic crochet uses a simple combination of single and double crochet stitches worked through the stitches in the row below to create a fabric with depth and a wonderful texture. Step-by-step instructions show how to work mosaic crochet, how to start a row, how to work both types of stitches, and how to finish a row in the mosaic crochet style.

Finishing techniques make a big difference to how your final project looks. Blocking a piece after you weave in all your yarn tails straightens its edges, smooths out its stitches, and makes your final piece beautiful.

Felting finished crochet projects is a fun way to completely change their texture. An easy technique for using a washing machine to felt a project is presented here to create firm and sturdy crochet pieces for pillows and rugs.

Abbreviations

Listed below are all the abbreviations that are used in the patterns throughout this book.

BLO	back loop only
CC	contrast color
ch	chain(s)
cm	centimeter(s)
dc	double crochet
FLO	front loop only
ft	feet
g	grams
hdc	half double crochet
in	inches
kg	kilograms
lb	pounds
m	meters
mm	millimeters
MC	main color
rep	repeat
RS	right side
sc	single crochet
skip	miss
sl st	slip stitch
st(s)	stitch(es)
WS	wrong side
yd	yard(s)
[ ]	repeat sequence in square brackets the number of times stated
*	repeat instructions following the * as directed

CROCHET TERMS

All the patterns in this book are written using US crochet terms. See below for equivalent UK terms.

US Term	UK Term
single crochet	double crochet
half double crochet	half treble crochet
double crochet	treble crochet
treble crochet	double treble crochet

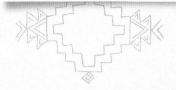

Basic Stitches

Here are step-by-step instructions for all the basic stitches, plus a few of the special stitches used in the projects.

Slip knot
Make a loop with the yarn tail hanging down. Insert the hook or your fingers in the loop and pull the working yarn through (A). Place onto the hook and pull to tighten (B).

Chain (ch)
Yarn over (C) and pull through a loop on the hook (D). Repeat to make as many chains as stated in the pattern.

Slip stitch (sl st)
Insert the hook into the stitch, yarn over (E), pull through both the stitch and the loop on the hook (F). The illustrations show a slip stitch joining the ends of a length of chain.

Front loop only (FLO) & back loop only (BLO)
The front loop is the loop closest to you; if the pattern says to crochet FLO, work the stitch into this loop only (G). The back loop is the one furthest from you; if the pattern says to crochet BLO, work the stitch into this loop only (H).

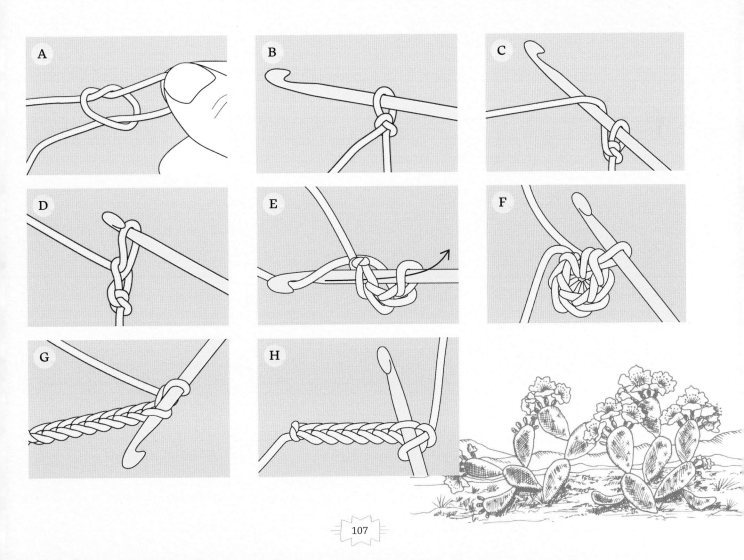

Single crochet (sc)

Insert the hook into the stitch or space, yarn over (I), and pull through the stitch or space (two loops on the hook), yarn over again, pull through both loops on the hook (J).

Half double crochet (hdc)

Yarn over, insert the hook into the stitch, yarn over, pull up a loop (three loops on the hook), yarn over (K) and pull through all three loops on the hook (L).

Double crochet (dc)

Yarn over, insert the hook into the stitch (M), yarn over and pull through the stitch (three loops on the hook) (N), yarn over, pull through the first two loops on the hook (two loops left on the hook) (O), yarn over and pull through the last two loops (P).

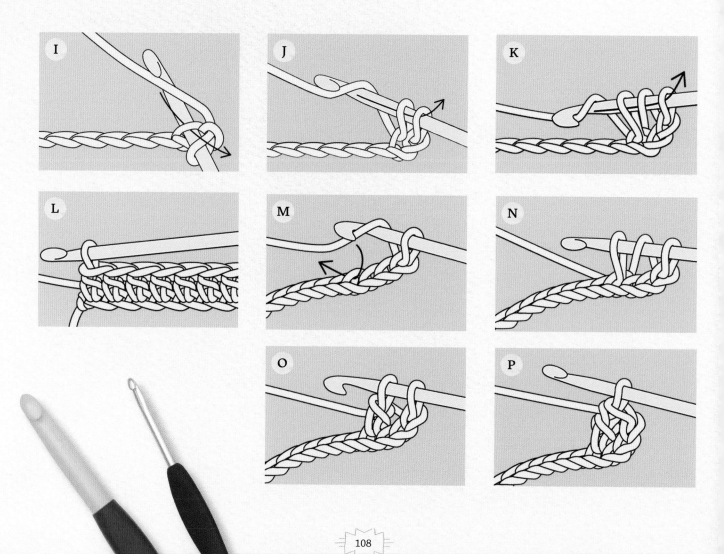

Bobble stitch

Yarn over, insert the hook into the stitch, yarn over and pull through the stitch, yarn over and pull through two loops (two loops on the hook), yarn over and insert the hook back into the same stitch (Q), yarn over and pull through the stitch, yarn over and pull through two loops (three loops on the hook), yarn over (R) and insert the hook into the same stitch, yarn over and pull through the stitch, yarn over and pull through two loops (four loops on the hook) (S), yarn over and insert the hook into the same stitch, yarn over and pull through the stitch, yarn over and pull through two loops (five loops on the hook), yarn over (T) and pull through all five loops on the hook (U). Single crochet into the next stitch. The bobble will puff out at the back of the work.

Reverse single crochet

Insert the hook in the stitch to the right (V), yarn over, pull through the stitch (W), yarn over, pull through both loops on the hook (X).

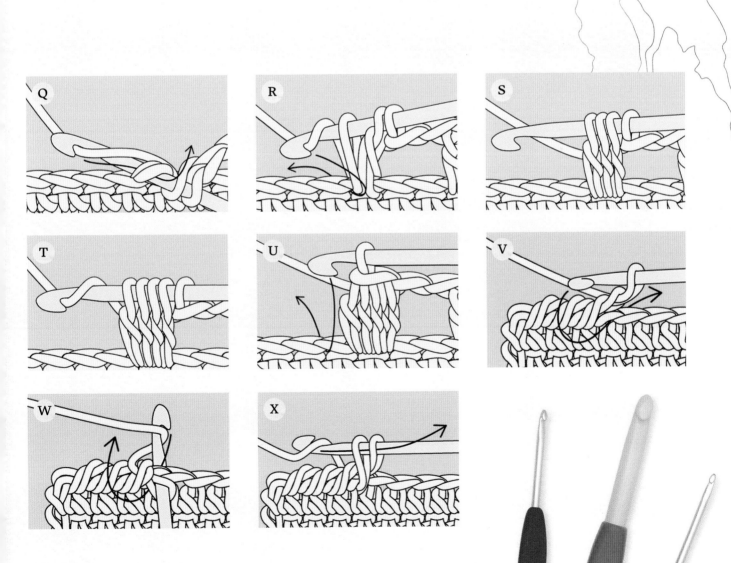

Borders & Fringes

Many crochet projects look great without a border. Striped projects like the Rio Grande Stripe Towels and the Land of Enchantment Blanket would lose their graphic punch if the vertical lines of a border crossed the flow of the horizontal stripes. If you are happy with your project without adding a border, feel free to leave it be!

BORDERS

Borders are useful for straightening any wobbly edges on a project and for hiding any yarn carried up the side edges of a colorwork project like the Canyon Moon Blanket and the Globe Trekker Throw. You can also cover the yarn ends created by overlay mosaic crochet, as in the Cactus Garden Blanket. Working a round of border around a pillow square also makes it easier to join the front and back squares evenly.

When working the border round along the edges of a single crochet project, work one border stitch into the end of each row. When working the border round along the edges of a double crochet project, work two border stitches into the end of each row, one into the top half of the double crochet stitch and one into the bottom half of the double crochet stitch (A). For the rest of the border rounds, work one single crochet stitch into each stitch (B).

For blanket borders, it is often best to use a crochet hook 1mm smaller than the hook used for the blanket to work the border round. This keeps the border round stitches small to prevent the border from becoming wavy. If the border round is wavy or ruffling, try a smaller crochet hook. If the border round is tight and curling inwards, try using the same crochet hook you used for the rest of the blanket.

FRINGES

A fringe will add a touch of fun and movement to your project.

Simple Yarn Tail Fringe

The very simplest fringe can be created by leaving long yarn tails at the start and end of each row. These can be knotted at the base, knotted at the end, or just trimmed to an even length.

Twisted Fringe

Twisted fringe can be created from yarn tails by twisting two tails or groups of tails in the same direction 20 or 30 times until the yarn begins to kink. Knot the ends of the tails together before letting go—the fringe will twist together when you let go. Trim the yarn tails to about ½in (1.3cm) below the knot.

A

B

Added Fringe

For a thicker, fuller fringed look, extra pieces of yarn can be added to the last row or round of a project to create clusters of fringes. One piece of yarn can be added to each stitch, or a group of three to six pieces of yarn can be added to each stitch.

To cut fringe, try wrapping yarn around a hardcover book. You can cut at just one end of the book to create long pieces or cut at both the top and bottom edges of the book to create shorter fringe pieces (A).

To add fringe, insert the hook into a stitch from the back of the work to the front. Fold a piece of yarn in half and grab the center with the hook (B). Pull the center of the folded yarn through the stitch just enough to tuck the free ends of the yarn through the folded loop (C). Pull to tighten (D).

Trim the fringe with your sharpest scissors. Trim straight across or create a zigzag if you like. Avoid tugging on the fringe as you trim because it may spring back to be shorter than you anticipate.

Macramé Fringe

Macramé fringe begins with adding fringes to the ends of a project as described in Added Fringe. Space each cluster of fringes four stitches apart (E). The cluster of fringes on each end of the fringed section should contain half the number of strands of the rest of the fringe clusters. For example, the cluster of fringes at each end could have six strands of yarn while the rest of the fringe clusters could have 12 strands of yarn.

Starting at the right-hand side of the project, tie all six strands of the end fringe with six strands from the next fringe to the left in a square knot (F, G) about 1in (2.5cm) below the project edge. Pull the knot tight. Repeat with the next fringe, tying the remaining six strands of the right-most fringe in a knot with six strands from the next fringe to the left (H). Repeat across the blanket on both ends and trim fringe as desired.

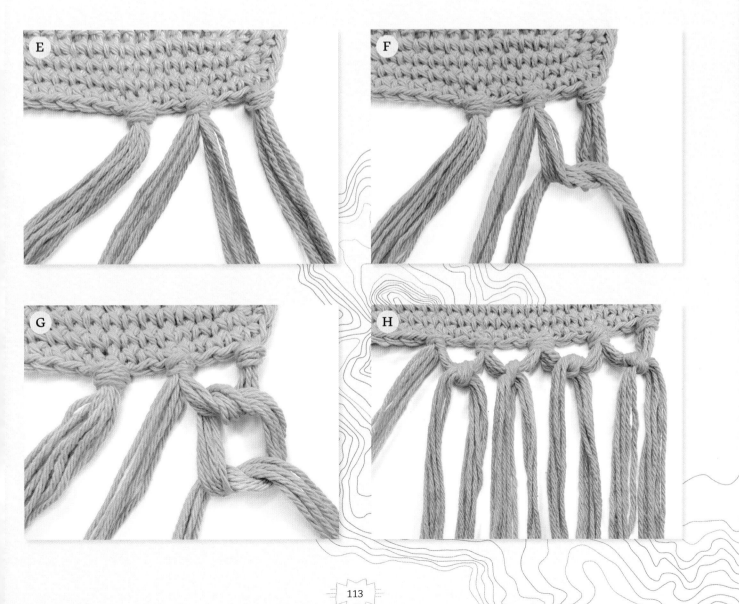

Layered Tassels

Making a layered tassel is just as easy as making a plain tassel; however, it can take some practice to keep the colors of the lower layers from showing through the top layer.

The shortest layer should contain the most pieces of yarn so it can cover the layers beneath it. The yarn for each layer should be about 4in (10cm) longer than the next shortest layer and should contain four to eight fewer pieces of yarn (I). Smooth each group of yarn pieces and trim the ends before you tie the tassel. This helps to keep the layers even and reduces the need for trimming.

Cut a length of yarn to use as a tie and lay it horizontally on a flat surface. Place the longest tassel pieces in the center of the tie piece vertically to form a cross shape. Place the medium tassel pieces on top. The shortest pieces will lay directly on top of the medium pieces. Knot the tie around all pieces to fasten (J, K).

Knot a long length of yarn around the top of the tassel to secure it (L), then wrap the yarn around the tassel top several times (M). Hide the end of the wrap yarn down inside the tassel using a yarn needle (N).

Comb through the tassel with your fingers to smooth the strands. Trim each tassel layer individually with your sharpest scissors. This step takes a bit of patience and time. Try using a yarn label wrapped around the end of the tassel to help you trim evenly. Attach a tassel to each corner of the project with a yarn needle or knot the tie ends around a basket or tote handle.

Making tassels takes practice. I often have to make five tassels to get four matching ones to add to a blanket. Use any leftover tassels for other projects or to decorate gifts.

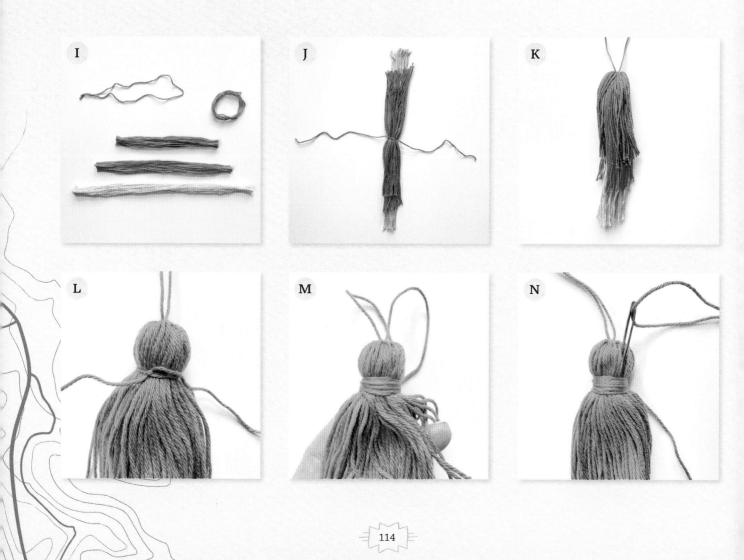

Tapestry Crochet

Tapestry crochet uses two or more colors of yarn in alternating sections to create colorful projects. Both sides of the fabric look the same—there is no right side or wrong side.

The terms "tapestry crochet" and "intarsia crochet" are often used interchangeably to mean crocheting with multiple colors in the same row. Tapestry crochet carries both the working and non-working yarns throughout the whole project. Intarsia crochet requires a separate ball of yarn for each color and does not carry yarn across the row. Both techniques are illustrated here.

Tapestry Crochet with Two Colors

In tapestry crochet with just two colors, such as a main color yarn and a contrast color yarn, both yarns can be carried throughout the whole project. This means that you can drop and pick up each color as needed, crocheting over the color you are not using to hide it inside the stitches. The carried yarn lies on top of the previous row of stitches and is hidden inside the stitches of the current row. This technique works especially well for projects that use double crochet stitches, like the Canyon Moon Blanket, the Globe Trekker Throw, and the Lone Mesa Pillows & Tote.

Preventing the Yarns from Tangling

The key to peaceful tapestry crochet is to keep the two yarns from tangling as you crochet. To do this, keep one ball of yarn in front and one ball in back at your side as you crochet. I like to keep the main color yarn next to me on the couch and the contrast color yarn on the floor at my feet while I crochet.

When you complete a section of one color yarn and pick up the new color, drop the old color yarn in the direction of its ball of yarn. I always drop the main color yarn toward the front of my work and drop the contrast color yarn to the back of my work. This keeps the yarn lines from getting crossed or wrapped around each other. If you always drop the yarn to the back of the work every time you change yarns, the two yarns will twist around each other and require untangling every few rows. Holding one yarn always toward the back of the work and the other yarn always toward the front prevents any tangles from forming in the first place and does not affect the look of the crocheted fabric.

Adding a New Color Yarn and Carrying Yarn

The second yarn color can be added at the beginning of a row or anywhere mid-row. To add a new color of yarn, yarn over with it to complete the last stitch of the first color (A) and pull through both loops on the hook (B). Gently tug both the old color yarn and the new color yarn to remove any slack. Crochet with the new color for as many stitches as required, laying the old color yarn over the top of the stitches from the previous row (C).

Crochet around the old color yarn to hide it inside the new color stitches (D). This is called "carrying yarn" because you are carrying it along as you crochet so you can pick it up again when the pattern requires it. I like to lay my carried yarn slightly to the front of the previous row (E). This hides it nicely inside the new stitches. If the carried yarn falls to the back of the work as it lays across the previous row, it can show through on the next row.

Changing Colors

Switch back to the first color by yarning over with it to complete the last stitch of the second color (F, G). Lay the first color yarn over the previous row and carry it along as you stitch with the second yarn color.

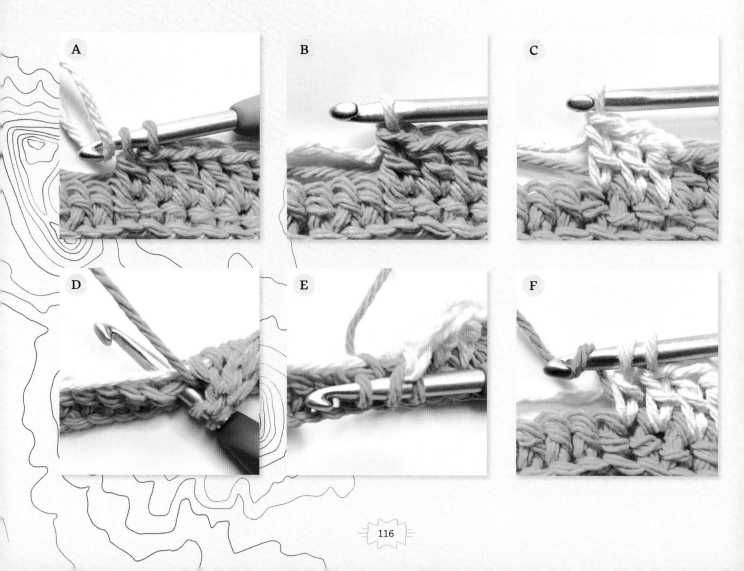

Carrying Yarn up the End of the Row

Carry both yarns up the end of each row by yarning over with the color you are not using to complete the last stitch (H, I). Then yarn over with the first yarn and pull through the loop on the hook (J). Tighten both yarns gently.

Starting the Next Row

To begin the next row, chain as the pattern requires (K) and pull the carried yarn up to lay on top of the previous row. Crochet around the yarn to hide it inside the row (L).

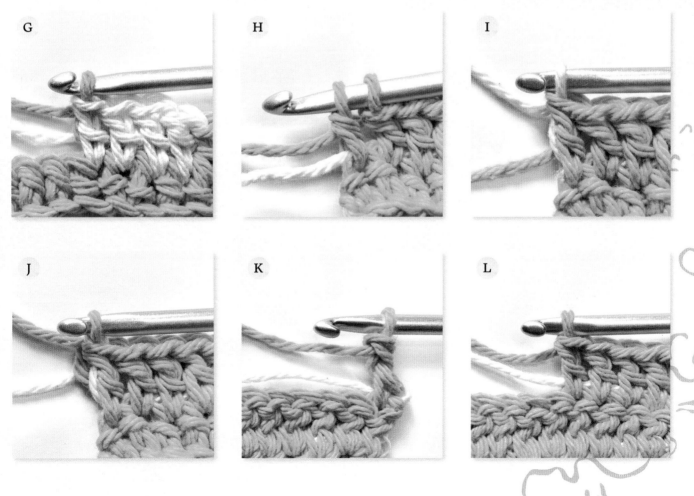

Color Show-Through

Some contrast color yarn showing through is normal, especially in sections of dark main color yarn with a very light contrast color. If you see too much contrast color yarn for your liking, try switching to a smaller crochet hook.

Tapestry Crochet with More Than Two Colors

When crocheting a project with more than two colors, I prefer to work each section of color from its own ball of yarn. I do not carry multiple colors of yarn across a row; instead, I drop and add each color as needed, letting the small balls of each color hang off the edge of the project as I work each row. This technique works well for both single crochet and double crochet projects, such as the Wind River Weighted Blanket and the Vallecito Blanket. You could also choose this method for an extra clean look in the Raider Ridge Wall Hangings or the Land of Enchantment Blanket & Pillow.

Before you begin, wind each color of yarn into several small balls. Create yarn balls about the size of an orange or a grapefruit to help keep yarn tangles to a minimum.

Adding a New Color Yarn at the Beginning of a Row

Yarn over with the new color (G) and pull through the loop on the hook (H). Then chain 1 or 3 as the pattern requires for single crochet or double crochet stitches (I). Gently tug both the old color yarn and the new color yarn to remove any slack. Crochet with the new color for as many stitches as required.

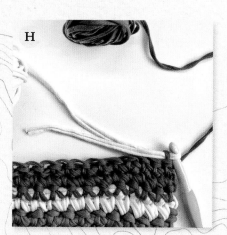

Changing Colors Mid-Row

To change to a new color, yarn over with the new color as the last yarn over of the last stitch in the old color (J). As you begin to stitch with the new color (K), leave the old color yarn behind by moving it to the back of the work (L). You will pick it back up in the next row.

Adding a New Color Mid-Row

Yarn over with the new color (M) using a new ball of that color to complete the last stitch of the old color (N). Drop the old color to the back of the work and crochet as many stitches in the new color as the pattern requires (O).

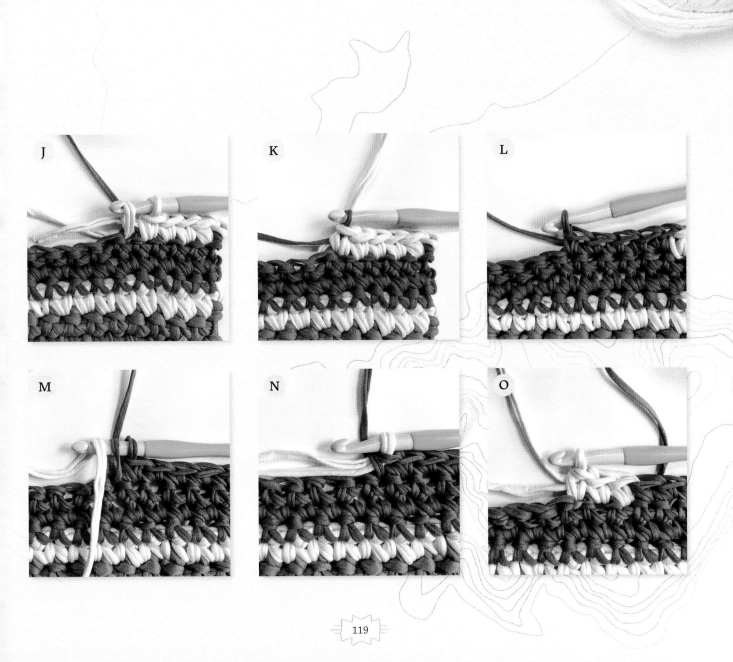

Managing the Balls of Yarn to Prevent Tangles

Your project will have a separate ball of yarn for each color hanging from the edge as you work. It takes a bit of experience to keep the yarns from tangling, but a few tricks can prevent tangles.

I find it helpful to keep the yarn balls on a tray or flat basket on a coffee table or foot stool in front of me. You can use a cardboard box to hold the balls of yarn in a neat row. You may find it more comfortable to put the box or tray on the floor in front of you. Keep the yarn balls in a row in the order that they are used in the pattern row. Drop the yarn to the back of the work when you are finished crocheting each section of color.

Turning the Work

The most important technique for preventing yarn tangles in multicolored projects is to alternate the way you turn your work at the end of each row. After the first row, turn the left-hand side of your project over to the right (P). After the next row, turn the right-hand side of your work over to the left (Q).

Give the yarn balls a little slack to unroll when you turn your work. The yarns will cross every other row (R). It might feel like they will tangle, but be patient! Leave the yarn balls in their line and let the yarns cross temporarily. They will uncross after the next row when you turn your work in the opposite direction (S). This technique works best when you keep the yarn balls in a box or tray in front of you, lined up in the order they are used in the pattern row.

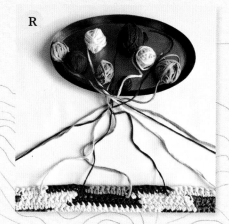

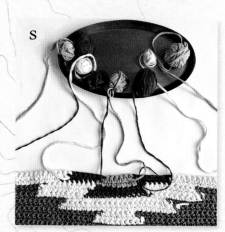

Picking Yarn Up in the Next Row

Sometimes you will need a color of yarn a few stitches earlier than where the yarn was dropped in the previous row. No need to cut the yarn; just pull the color over to where you need it (T). Give it enough slack so that it doesn't pull your stitches tight or out of shape, but give it a gentle tug to prevent a loose loop hanging out between stitches (U). Crochet over the yarn to hide the pulled section of yarn inside the stitches.

You may need a color only one stitch earlier than the previous row. In this case, you will pull the yarn over only one stitch to the right (V). Crochet over the short pulled section of yarn for two stitches for a clean color change (W, X, Y).

If you need a color later than the previous row, you can pick the yarn up and carry it until you need it by crocheting around it.

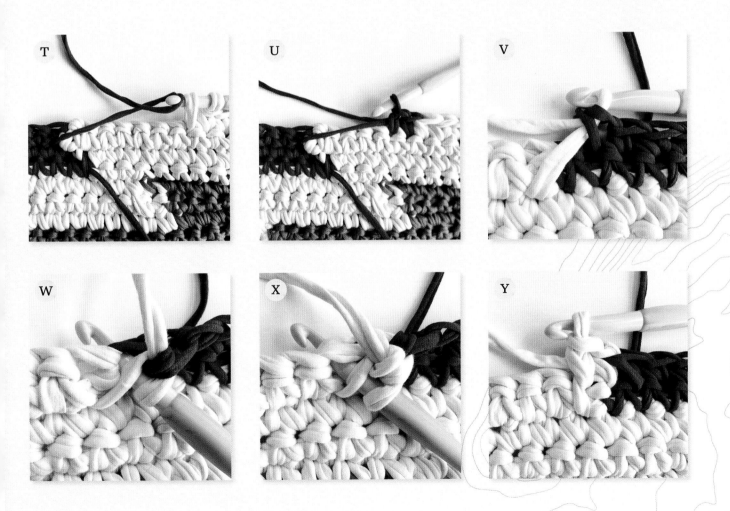

Mosaic Crochet

Mosaic crochet creates geometric patterns using only one color of yarn at a time. The patterns in this book use the overlay mosaic crochet technique in which the yarn is cut after each row.

In overlay mosaic crochet, the yarn color changes after each row. Odd rows (Row 1, Row 3, Row 5, and so on) are always worked using the main color (MC) yarn. These rows form the diamond pattern of the Cactus Garden Blanket and the zigzag path of the Dreamer's Path Wrap. I like to use a lighter color for the MC yarn.

Even rows (Row 2, Row 4, Row 6, and so on) are always worked using the contrast color (CC) yarn. I like to use a darker yarn color for these rows to make the lighter main color rows and pattern pop. Even rows are all the same: single crochet through the back loop only of each stitch across. The only exception is the first and last stitch of each row, which are worked through both loops of the stitch.

Do not turn your work after each row. Instead, always work from right to left and keep the same side of the blanket facing you (the front or right side). Left-handed crocheters will always work from left to right.

When you begin each row, attach your yarn leaving a long tail. Cut the yarn at the end of each row leaving a long tail and fasten off by pulling the end through the loop on your hook.

If you would rather make fringe than cover the yarn ends with a border, join the yarn with a 12in (30.5cm) tail and leave a 12in (30.5cm) tail at the end of each row. If you are not sure at this stage whether you want fringe or a border, leave long tails just in case.

To start each row, attach the yarn with a slip stitch into the first stitch on the right-hand edge of your work (A). Chain 1, then single crochet through both loops of the first stitch (B, C), the same stitch where you joined the yarn. Then single crochet through the back loop only of the next stitch (D, E).

Each row will end as it began—with a single crochet stitch through the back loop only of the second-to-last stitch and a single crochet stitch through both loops of the last stitch.

Odd rows include some double crochet stitches to create the raised pattern. These double crochet stitches are worked into the row below the one you would normally stitch into (F). You are double crocheting into the previous odd row (the previous MC row).

Your double crochet stitches will lay in front of your work (G, H), creating a little gap or space at the back where you skipped the CC stitches (I).

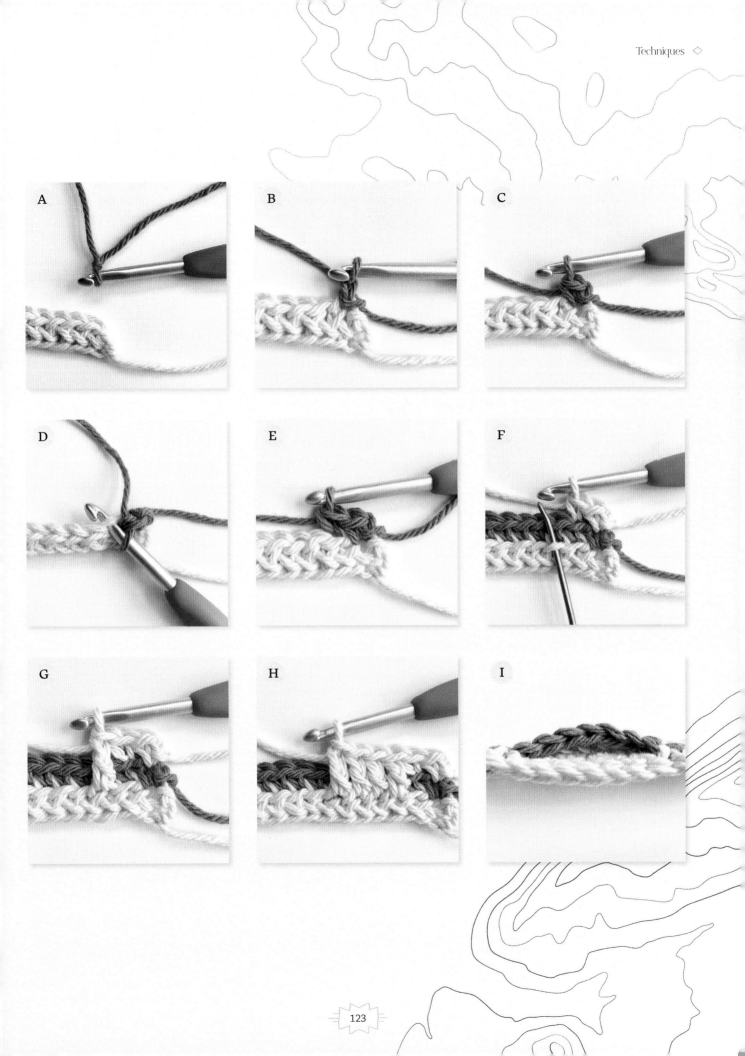

A

B

C

D

E

F

G

H

I

Blocking & Finishing

Blocking is a way to even out the stitches and edges of your projects. Take your time when weaving in yarn tails. Securing yarn ends neatly will give your work a professional look and help it to last for years to come.

BLOCKING

The basic technique of blocking is to get the project wet, smooth it out into the ideal shape, pin the edges down, and allow it to dry. If you are happy with the shape of your project as it is, then feel free to skip blocking.

I use foam children's play mats as my blocking surface, but you can substitute a few layers of old towels on the floor or a towel over a mattress. Let the project soak in cool water in a sink or tub for a few minutes, then squeeze out the excess water. Spend a minute or two smoothing and stretching the project into shape, evening out the edges. You can use a tape measure to be sure the project is smoothed into a symmetrical shape. Pin the edges of the project to the blocking surface. You can use any pins as long as they are not rusty, or blocking combs like Knitter's Pride Knit Blockers. Allow the piece to dry completely before removing the pins.

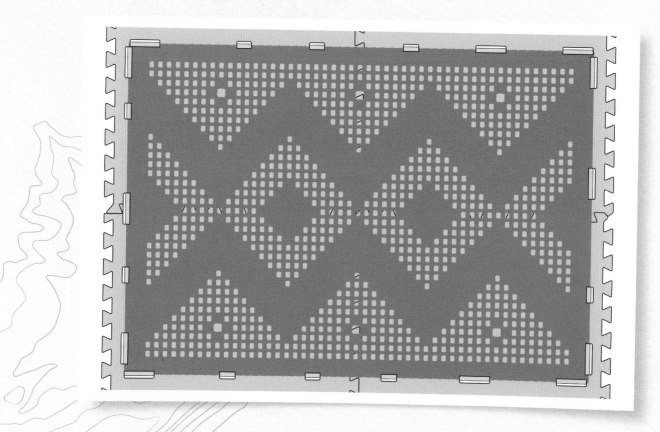

WEAVING IN YARN ENDS

Leave a 4–6in (10–15cm) yarn tail when starting a project, adding a new color, or cutting yarn to fasten off. Using a tapestry needle, draw the yarn tail through the center of four or five stitches (A). Then insert the needle one stitch back from where the yarn tail came out (B). Thread the needle forward through four or five more stitches (C). Carefully trim the yarn tail close to the project (D).

When using bulky or super bulky yarn, it is easier to use a small hook to weave in the yarn ends than it is to thread the thick yarn through a tapestry needle. Insert the hook under a few stitches, grab the yarn end with the hook (E), and pull the yarn end through the stitches (F). Repeat as needed.

FELTING

Felting is a fun way to completely transform the look and texture of a project. It can also help to tighten loose stitches or even out wobbly edges. Choose 100% wool yarn for a project that you plan to felt. Navajo Churro and old Spanish Churro yarns will both felt very nicely.

Weave in the yarn ends of your project. Wash in a washing machine with hot water. I like to add a few old towels to the washing machine along with my project to help agitate it. Tumble dry on the highest temperature setting available. Wash again in the washing machine with hot water but this time leave it wet. Smooth the project into an even shape and pin it to a blocking mat or a layer of towels to dry. When assembling two felted squares to make a pillow, it's easier to use a sewing needle and thread than to crochet through both felted pieces. You can also sew one felted rectangle or square onto an old fabric cushion cover to make something new.

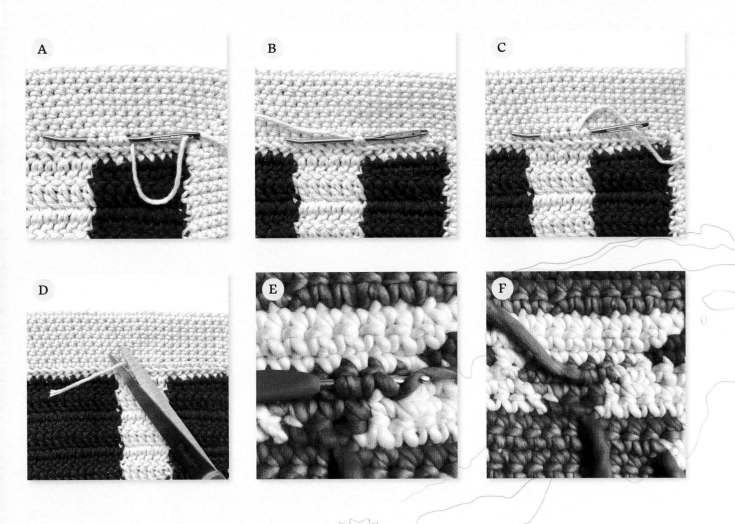

ABOUT THE AUTHOR

Susan Kennedy lives in the mountains of southwest Colorado with her husband and three sons. She earned a bachelor's degree in mathematics and biology and a Ph.D. in neuroscience from the University of Michigan before she learned to crochet. She hooked her first projects in 2012 while traveling the US in a vintage Volkswagen camper van. When she's not teaching science to university students or crocheting on her front porch, you can find her hiking, camping, snowboarding, or paddleboarding with her family.

Pretty Peaceful crochet design was born in 2013 as a fundraising effort for the Kentucky Birth Coalition. Susan opened the Pretty Peaceful Etsy shop to help pass legislation to grant licenses to certified professional midwives. In 2019, the Coalition achieved their goal and licensed certified professional midwives now bring maternity care to the families of Kentucky. The Pretty Peaceful Etsy shop continues to fundraise with the goal of changing Kentucky law to allow midwives to open licensed freestanding birth centers.

Pretty Peaceful patterns and tutorials have been published in most popular crochet magazines as well as on Ravelry, LoveCrafts, Etsy, and YouTube. Learn more at **www.prettypeaceful.com.**

SUPPLIERS

Dibe' be' iina (Sheep is Life)
Navajo Nation Navajo Churro wool
www.dibebeiina.etsy.com
Email: benallyart@yahoo.com
Joe Benally P.O. Box 615, Pinon, AZ

Four Corners Yarns
4405 S. Lance Road, Flagstaff, AZ
86005

Freia Fine Handpaints
www.freiafibers.com
Phone: +1-510-599-1385
Email: studio@freiafibers.com
60 Roberts Drive, Suite 204, North
Adams, MA 01247

Hobbii
www.hobbii.com
Phone: +1-888-557-9710
Email: support@hobbii.com
Copenhagen, Denmark

Hoooked
www.hooookedyarn.com
Phone: +351 249 248 796
Rua das Matas 4, 2350-818
Zibreira, Portugal

Knit Picks
www.knitpicks.com
Phone: 080-8234-6084126
P.O. Box 87760, Vancouver, WA
98687-7760

Lion Brand Yarn
www.lionbrand.com
Phone: +1-800-661-7551
Email:
support@email.lionbrand.com
135 Kero Road, Carlstadt,
NJ 07072, USA

Malabrigo
www.malabrigoyarn.com
Phone US: +1-786-427-1048
Phone Europe: +44-20-3514-1551
Email: europa@malabrigoyarn.com
Uruguay and Peru

Rowan Yarn
www.knitrowan.com
Flanshaw Lane, Wakefield, WF2
9ND, West Yorkshire UK

Shepherd's Lamb
www.organiclamb.com
Phone: +1-505-795-3671
Email: shepherd@organiclamb.com
2540 US Hwy 64
Chama, NM 87520 USA

Yarnspirations
www.yarnspirations.com
Phone: 1-888-368-8401
Email: inquire@yarnspirations.com
North America

INDEX

Thanks

I would like to thank my family and friends for their loving support. My twin sister Karen von Kluge for her good advice, time, and expertise in crochet and editing. My husband Aaron our chief transportation officer and my sons Will, Rider, and Luke for their loving support. Thank you to Donna Lightning Feather Brown for inspiration, photography, and modeling, and to Rachel Jenkin for always being up for a road trip. Thank you to Hooooked, Malabrigo, Hobbii, and Knit Picks for generously providing yarn support. Thank you to Ame, Lucy, Anna, Jeni, and the rest of the creative team at David and Charles. Thank you to my parents, may they rest in peace, and to all of my ancestors whose love made my life possible.

A DAVID AND CHARLES BOOK
© David and Charles, Ltd 2023

David and Charles is an imprint of David and Charles, Ltd
Suite A, Tourism House, Pynes Hill, Exeter, EX2 5WS

Text and Designs © Susan Kennedy 2023
Layout and Photography © David and Charles, Ltd 2023

First published in the UK and USA in 2023

A catalogue record for this book is available from the
British Library.

ISBN-13: 9781446309407 paperback
ISBN-13: 9781446381908 EPUB
ISBN-13: 9781446310489 PDF

This book has been printed on paper from approved suppliers and
made from pulp from sustainable sources.

Printed in the UK by Buxton for:
David and Charles, Ltd
Suite A, Tourism House, Pynes Hill, Exeter, EX2 5WS

10 9 8 7 6 5 4

Publishing Director: Ame Verso
Managing Editor: Jeni Chown
Editor: Jessica Cropper
Project Editor: Marie Clayton
Head of Design: Anna Wade
Art Direction and Design: Lucy Ridley
Pre-press Designer: Ali Stark
Illustrations: Kuo Kang Chen
Photography: Cole Davis, Jason Jenkins and Donna
Lightning Feather
Model: Camille Davis
Production Manager: Beverley Richardson

David and Charles publishes high-quality books on a wide range
of subjects. For more information visit www.davidandcharles.com.

Share your makes with us on social media using #dandcbooks
and follow us on Facebook and Instagram by searching
for @dandcbooks.

Layout of the digital edition of this book may vary depending on
reader hardware and display settings.

Image Credits

P.7: Images of Navajo Churro sheep courtesy of Joe Benally at the Dibe' be' iina Ranch
P.10-11: Images courtesy of Tierra Wools
P.16: Breanna Galley on Unsplash
P.24: Colin Lloyd on Unsplash
P.36: Robert Penaloza on Unsplash
P.42: Bryan Woolbright on Unsplash
P.52: John Fowler on Unsplash
P.53: 2 Bull Photography on Unsplash
P.56: John Fowler (left) and Lauren Thimmesch (right) on Unsplash
P.60: John Fowler on Unsplash
P.78: Cullen Jones on Unsplash
P.92: Aveedibya Dey Gat on Unsplash
P.97: Ganapathy Kumar on Unsplash